ANYTHING IS POSSIBLE

How a **former nun** counseled **drug addicts**, worked in **machine shops**, survived a **serial killer**, became a **spiritual teacher** and **publisher** – and what this means for **You!**

by KRYSTA GIBSON

ANYTHING IS POSSIBLE

How a former nun counseled drug addicts, worked in machine shops, survived a serial killer, became a spiritual teacher and publisher – and what this means for You!

by KRYSTA GIBSON

Book cover and book design by Rhonda Dicksion, www.indigodog.com

Copyright©2015 by Krysta Gibson. Published and distributed in the United States of America by Silver Owl Publications. All rights reserved. No part of this book may be reproduced by any mechanical, photographic, or electronic process, nor may it be stored in a retrieval system, transmitted, or otherwise copied for public or private use – other than for "fair use" as brief quotations embodied in articles and reviews – without prior written permission of the publisher.

Tradepaper ISBN: 978-1-879375-04-8

Other books by Krysta Gibson
Comments on Leading the Spiritual Life
22 Steps to Success
Business Success for Body, Mind, & Spirit
How to Get Your Article Printed in a Magazine or Newspaper
22 Pasos Hacia El Exito (en español)
Las Herramientas del Emprendedor (en español)

Courses, guided meditations, and self-talk MP3s can be found at www.krystagibson.com

Read New Spirit Journal at www.newspiritjournal.com

Silver Owl Publications
Monroe, Washington
www.anoasisforyoursoul.com

First Printing June 2015
Printed in the United States of America
Silver Owl Publications is a women owned and operated company.

What people are saying about Anything is Possible!

Krysta Gibson's book, *Anything is Possible*, is so much more than a memoir. While funny, entertaining — even shocking in parts — it is really a guidebook for living your own best life. It reads like a good novel; finding myself eager to turn each page, and having to continually remind myself that these are true revelations from an amazing life well-lived. Without any "preaching" whatsoever there is still a life-affirming lesson on virtually every page.

With the added bonus of the "rest stops" along Krysta's journey, you get a chance to stop and ponder what she just revealed. And a revelation it truly is! By the end you'll be saying, "If Krysta could do all of this — and survive it — then anything is possible for me."

— Marty Marsh, Soul Proprietor and marketing coach

If this quote from the book blows your hair back...

"You show me one machine in this shop that it takes a penis to run and I will walk out of here and never come back."

...be prepared for a delightful ride! I've been reading metaphysical/spiritual books for over 50 years and Krysta Gibson's book, *Anything is Possible* has a sauciness and 21st century life utility that charms, delights, and goes down as smoothly as Godiva chocolate.

It is not just a book of how her life has played out so far, it is a "how-to" manual for living well. I want a copy for my own library so I can refer back to her wise "Rest Stops." Buy it. Buy two and give one to a young person starting out the long journey in adult life. Some day they will thank you for it.

— Trisha Mahi, medium and author, Kona, Hawaii

So here's the thing about *Anything is Possible*... it's like a fictional portrayal of a spiritual being becoming aware of being human in the midst of a life filled with difficult obstacles and sometimes excruciatingly arduous circumstances... only to triumph in the end with a strength of spirit we can only wish we had. But, paraphrasing an old saying, the truth is sometimes stranger, and certainly more uplifting, than fiction. Krysta Gibson and her true life story are both the truth of a well-lived spiritual experience on the human side of the line and an inspiration to the rest of us.

— Rob Spears and Brenda Michaels, Conscious Talk Radio

Krysta's journey is the tale of an American woman of our generation in search of freedom, in search of herself, eager to be of service to others, willing to risk all, and seeking true, unconditional love and friendship! Hers is the adventure of a soul seeking the Light.

— Nayaswami Hriman McGilloway, Ananda Church of Self-Realization

Inspiring memoir of living a dream with courage and joy.
— Robbie Holz, author of *Secrets of Aboriginal Healing* and *Aboriginal Secrets of Awakening*

Everyone's life journey comes with its dramas. Most of us dare not to share our deepest moments of growth because of the pain of memory. Krysta, however, does. An accomplished professional, she wants you to know that you can travel your journey with power, presence, and purpose. Also, you can enjoy rest stops along the way so you can see the greatness in your experiences and change direction if you want to.
— Donna Seebo, psychic, medium, and radio talk show host.

If you ever get discouraged and think that some goal of yours cannot be attained or accomplished, this book is for you. Well-written and easily read, Krysta will inspire you with her spiritual wisdom, insight, and guidance. Through captivating stories of her own experience, she shows us that miracles do happen and truly, *Anything Is Possible*!
— Martha Norwalk, host of Martha Norwalk's Animal World

Krysta Gibson has lived a powerful and adventurous life, following guidance, living on faith, and gifting humanity in the process through her many ventures. Her book gives us a glimpse of her life and how we, too, can open to this trust and guidance and move toward living fearlessly, embracing our true path and mission. A must-read for anyone wanting to consciously embrace these powerful times of planetary transformation.
— Katelon T. Jeffereys

Anything is Possible **is a fascinating, adventure-filled account of Krysta Gibson's life.** Her inspirational and poignant stories mirror our own soul's search for comfort, clarity, and validation and opens a space for us to courageously face life's challenges with confidence, ease, and grace.
— Gianna Moriah Rosewood, M.A., CCHT, LMP,
  co-author of the book, *Are You Still Kissing Frogs?*

Anything Is Possible **is an entertaining and amazingly true story of one woman's path to deep wisdom.** Through her own lessons and with light-heartedness, Gibson gently guides us to step into our fullest potential.
— Christine Upchurch, director, Stellar Reflections,
  and host of The Christine Upchurch Show

I am amazed at Krysta's determination to create what she wanted in life. As she shares her story you feel her strength as a woman. She said yes to what her spirit was calling for next and didn't let others stop her from her goals. As we follow her spiritual journey; we witness how she reached for her dreams and achieved who she is today: a role model for anyone searching for answers to what is next in their lives. From being a nun, counselor, machinist, newspaper publisher, writer, and more, Krysta shares her stories of failures and successes. She asks challenging questions to address the issues that impact our lives and gives tools on how to live on purpose. Krysta allowed herself to be vulnerable in sharing her life with us and she will inspire you to create the life you dream of… today!
— Kris Steinnes, founder of Women of Wisdom Foundation and author of
  Women of Wisdom, Empowering the Dreams and Spirit of Women.

Contents

Introduction 11
Chapter 1:   The Beginning 13
Chapter 2:   My Early Years 15
Chapter 3:   I Go To The Convent 25
Chapter 4:   Life In The Convent 29
Chapter 5:   Leaving The Convent 39
Chapter 6:   Life After The Covent 43
Chapter 7:   Washing The Nun Out of Me 47
Chapter 8:   The Puppy Chapter 49
Chapter 9:   Learning About Life 55
Chapter 10: Women Don't Cut Iron... Or Do They? 67
Chapter 11: How I Met A Serial Killer
                    and Lived to Tell About It 71
Chapter 12: Gullible's Trabbels 75
Chapter 13: Bouncing Around and Finding My Place ... 79
Chapter 14: The Reawakening 83
Chapter 15: Learning How to Run a Small Newspaper .. 91
Chapter 16: My Future is Revealed 95
Chapter 17: The New Times is Born 99
Chapter 18: The Early Days 105
Chapter 19: People Stepped Up to Help Me 119
Chapter 20: I Sell My Baby 123
Chapter 21: Caring For Our Elders 127
Chapter 22: New Spirit Journal is Born 129
Chapter 23: Let's Network! 133
Chapter 24: Voy a España 135
Chapter 25: My Brother Dies 139
Chapter 26: Gurus 149
Afterword or What A Journey We've Been On! 155
Acknowledgements 157

Dedicated to my brother Louis J. Gibson
Keep the rainbows coming!

Introduction

Y ou want to believe that anything is possible in your life. You want to open your heart and mind to the idea that life offers much more than what you have experienced so far. This is why you're reading this book. This is what I want for you and it's why I'm writing this book. I hope that by sharing some of the stories and lessons of my life, you will be inspired to live more fully and make the most of the life you've been given. Truthfully, anything is possible!

This has not been an easy book to write because I'm a very private person. I don't like talking about myself and rarely do I reveal the depths of what I'm thinking or feeling. I have dragged my feet and have found all sorts of good reasons not to work on this project. My ego asks, "What will people think of me when they find out more about who I am and some of the things that have happened in my life?"

Divine guidance, however, steps in and says, "That doesn't matter. Your stories and lessons will inspire, entertain, and encourage others. You must write the book."

Like an overstuffed armchair, my life has been filled with improbable events, people, and circumstances. Often, I have felt that I have lived several lifetimes within this one. It's as if I have been trying to tie up loose ends with thousands of souls while experiencing as many different facets of life on this planet as I can.

What this means is I have had the good fortune to meet and interact with a wide variety of people - from those I would consider saintly to those I would call evil. And I have interacted with hundreds of everyday people like myself. At times, I have lived a very spiritually-based lifestyle and at others I have lived a very earthly one. Both have taught me a lot.

There's a thread that runs through my life as it does yours. I believe we are souls who incarnate here in order to learn who and what we really are. Everything and everyone who crosses our path does so for a reason. It is up to us to be aware and figure out what the reason is and then use it to our advantage and growth.

Like the sunflower blooming in the darkness of night on the cover of this book, we can blossom in the midst of life's challenges.

This book contains various stories about my life. Everything here is true to the best of my recollection. In general, I have not used real names of people who are still living unless they are public figures of some kind or I was able to get their permission. The reason for this is because I don't have permission from the other people to tell their parts of the stories and, in most cases, have no idea how to find them to ask their permission. In other situations, I have not told the entire story and there are some events I don't tell at all. I want to be sensitive not only to myself but to other people.

At no time do I want to embarrass anyone – myself or others – so I have simply omitted anything I thought would not contribute to your upliftment or education. If you know me personally and notice that I have not told a story you think I should have told, especially if it involves you, accept my apologies. Anything I left out, I did so out of sensitivity, not because you or the event was unimportant.

At intervals, I have Rest Stops. These are places where we'll pull off to the side of the road and you'll be given the chance to reflect and apply the information to your own life. It's fun to read about other people and how they have lived. It's even more fun to ponder how we can apply what they learned to our own lives. This is the purpose of the Rest Stops.

Now let's get started on the journey. Hop aboard with me as I share how I learned anything – yes, anything – is possible, not only in my life but in yours.

Krysta Gibson
Summer Solstice, 2015

The beginning.

One day, I picked up the telephone in my office, called my boss, and said, "This is my one-month notice. I'm quitting my job and moving to Seattle to start a monthly New Age community newspaper." I hung up the phone and asked myself, "What did I just do? I have no money to start a business, only nine months experience working at a newspaper, know two people in Seattle, and have barely enough money to move and virtually none to support myself."

But move I did. I started a newspaper called The New Times, built it to have a readership of over 40,000 people, operated it for 11 years, and sold it for just under six digits. This was before the days of computers in every business and home, the internet, or cell phones.

Since then I have worked in other businesses, started a second publication called New Spirit Journal and, with my spouse, operate these plus a web design business, write books, make guided meditation audios, give classes, and operate a mentoring and consulting business.

Over the years, people have asked me how I did this and how I continue to do so many different things. When I tell parts of my story in classes and workshops, people say it inspires them to follow their dreams. The time has come to share these tales with a wider audience.

The story begins where all good stories start: the beginning. Who am I? Where did I come from? And a question I have been asked many times: what did I do before the age of 38 when I began The New Times?

My early years.

We are all shaped by the families into which we're born. Whether our parents truly loved one another and wanted this new child in their world matters. The sort of economic world we enter makes a difference. The educational level and careers of our parents, geographical location, world events, spirituality in the home or lack thereof, all of this makes a difference in who we grow up to be.

I believe in reincarnation. Nothing else makes sense to me. I believe we arrive here with our own stories, our own baggage, and our own agenda. We don't consciously know this as babies, and even as adults much of this remains a mystery.

This matters because our abilities to create and manifest, to be the sort of person we think we want to be, are partially shaped by our early childhood as well as by our past lives. Knowing this makes accomplishing our life's work easier.

For me, this is hindsight. I didn't grow up believing in reincarnation and I didn't grow up knowing my future was being greatly influenced by the events of my childhood and by my past lives. My story begins in the fall of the late 1940s in south Texas.

World War II had ended and life was beginning to improve for many people. Unemployment in the United States was at 3.9% and a first-class letter could be mailed for only three cents.

My dad was a carpenter and he, along with my school teacher mother, two older brothers, and my sister, were just finishing building the house I was to grow up in.

People always want to know how many brothers and sisters I have and this gets complicated. My father was married to another woman before he married my mother. His first wife died. From that marriage, he had a girl and two boys.

Later, my Dad married my mother and they had two little boys who both died, one at birth and one after about a year. My mother had what is called the RH-negative factor and was told not to have any more children for fear they would not survive. Wanting another child and being Catholics, my parents were able to adopt a boy with the help of the parish priest.

About two years later, my mother got pregnant and had another boy. The doctors told her to stop getting pregnant. Using the great rhythm method, I came along two years later. (Joke: "What do they call people who use the rhythm method of birth control? Mommy and Daddy.")

The first group of two boys and a girl, my half-brothers and half-sister, were teenagers by the time I came along. The boys had left home and my sister left home when I was four. Effectively, I was raised with two brothers, one three years older and one two years older.

You can see how complicated it is to respond to the simple question of how many children were in my family!

I was born by Cesarean section and had to stay in an incubator for the first few weeks of my life. Due to the RH-negative factor, I had several blood transfusions shortly after birth.

Once I began my metaphysical spiritual path many years later, I realized I must not have been very happy to find myself in a body and was trying to decide to stay or go in those first few weeks. This has been borne out by astrologers who have read my chart. They say that once I was here, I wasn't sure I wanted to go through with this lifetime and wavered about staying.

I also realize that this started off my life path without the benefits that come from a trouble-free birth and it must have been really difficult for me as a baby not to be held and nurtured those first few weeks.

Most likely, this accounts for my being able to enjoy being alone as well as being fairly independent. I think it also accounts for my ability to be pretty detached from people and situations when I want to be.

If you were born Cesarean or you're in relationship with someone who was, I encourage you to read *Different Doorway: Adventures of a Cesarean Born* by Jane English (1985). There can be habits, personality traits, and expectations unique to people with this experience. Of interest is that more babies are being delivered this way than ever before, and I am not sure this is such a good idea.

I am eternally grateful to my mother for instilling in me a love for reading and learning. I am eternally grateful to my father for teaching me a strong work ethic and for letting me, a girl child of the 1950s, help him fix cars and build things. I know how to handle a screwdriver and hammer and wrenches. You'll see why this is important later in my story.

I was a religious child. I loved church. I loved Jesus and Mary and the saints. I went to Catholic Mass every day, even during the summer when I didn't have to go. I would walk to church on my own when no one in my family who drove a car wanted to go.

Great peace would come to me when I was in our local church, kneeling and saying the rosary or reading from my prayer book. Church was a haven for my young soul, a place I could rest from life and a place I experienced as home.

From the age of four, I said I wanted to be a nun. Sometimes I varied from this and said I wanted to be a nurse or teacher, but most of the time I wanted to become a nun.

Because my mom wanted to get back to her teaching job after being pregnant with me, I started first grade at the age of four. Kindergarten didn't exist then and my parents knew the nuns who taught at our local school. My mom was going to be teaching there, so the school bent the rules and I was five when it was time to begin second grade.

I still have my report card from

In the Catholic Church the day of one's First Communion is a very special day as it is when one takes the "body" of Christ for the first time. I wore this same outfit several other times when I was a flower girl for various church events.

that year. I made all "A's" except for a "C" in arithmetic. However, because I was only five and the rules had just been changed dictating that children had to be six to start first grade, it was decided to hold me back a year.

Believe it or not, the school made me repeat first grade because of the new rule. When I moved ahead to the second grade, I was still younger than my classmates.

Sometimes I've wondered if this gave me some sort of complex. Did it make me feel I can't succeed even when I do things right? Did it leave me feeling insecure?

Or did it give me the stick-to-it-tiveness it takes to keep going no matter what? And did it help me have some humility? Did it help me know how to deal as an equal with people older than myself?

Truthfully, it did all of these things.

This was probably my first major opportunity to continue on in the face of adversity, a trait that has served me well over the years.

There were all sorts of challenges with my mother teaching at the same grade school my brothers and I attended. Other kids thought we were the favored ones because our mom was at school with us all day. We didn't feel that way at all. We felt we couldn't get away from her anywhere!

I was in my mother's class for sixth grade and it was horrible. Not only did I have to call her Mrs. Gibson, but she was tougher on me than on the other students. She didn't want them to think she was playing favorites, so she was stricter with me.

I understood her logic, but it was still one of the most difficult school years I ever had.

The benefits of having a school teacher as a mother

One of the biggest benefits to having a school teacher as a mother is that I was raised in an educational environment. I began reading at the age of four and some books were way beyond my years. *A Tale of Two Cities* was one of the books I remember reading as a child. I doubt I understood everything in the many books I read, but it gave me a great vocabulary. And I am a very fast reader which has served me well in my capacity as a book reviewer for my newspapers.

When my brothers and I were out of school for the summer, so was our mother. So although I missed having a stay-at-home mom who baked cookies and took care of the home while I was at school, I had a mom who had the summers and holidays off when I did.

I had a mom who encouraged me to do science experiments. We bought an egg incubator and tried to hatch an egg. I had a microscope from a young age, did science experiments of various kinds, and kept bird, flower, and insect journals, carefully noting each variety I ever saw.

And the animals we had, oh my. My first dog was a white Spitz mix we got from the pound or animal shelter. I was creative in the naming process and called him Whitie. He and I were great pals. I taught him all sorts of tricks including how to climb a ladder!

In those days, most dogs lived outside. Ours was no exception and my father was dead set against allowing the dog in the house. Whitie lived outside chained to his dog house. The chain was long enough for him to get up on top of the flat roof and move around, but he was still on a chain.

Whitie was my first dog and we spent many happy hours together. I taught him tricks, even how to climb a ladder.

I walked him twice a day and eventually took him for runs while I rode my bike. He didn't have a bad life. And every now and then when my father was gone, somehow or another Whitie would find his way into the house and have a great time running around until my mother made me take him back outside.

He was not neutered. Every once in awhile he would get loose and take off down the street looking for a girlfriend. Instead, he would usually find the big male Chow dog who lived down the street and who was always loose. They would get into the worst fights, growling and struggling with one another as I would come running up to them, trying to get them free of each other.

Usually, without the help of an adult, I succeeded, took my dog back home and tried to make sure he couldn't get loose again. It is amazing that I was not bitten by either dog.

I detest dogs living outside. I would rather not have a dog at all than relegate them to the outside. Dogs are part of the family and I'm glad people are finally beginning to realize this. I know some people don't like having dog fur in the house. I always say if you don't like dog fur, you shouldn't have a dog.

Dogs are our friends, confidants, and angels. They belong in the house, and they should be neutered or spayed.

Let's talk cats

My brother Lou was the cat person in the household. He and my mother loved a finicky Siamese cat named Skunerell, whose name, they said, was French for "scoundrel."

We didn't allow him to run outside freely. When he went outdoors, he had to be on a leash. When he was going to stay outside for awhile we had him on a longer leash and tied him to a tree or a post on the porch.

One day I had taken him outside on our front porch. I don't know what spooked him, but something did and he turned around and climbed me like I was a tree. I had deep scratch marks from my eyes all the way down my left leg. I was a bloody mess and caused quite a stir when I ran back in the house without the cat, blood flowing.

I am sure I should have had stitches, but my parents didn't believe in going to doctors so they fixed me up and used hydrogen peroxide to clean out the wounds. No tetanus shot, either. I was a lucky girl and survived with scars that I have to this day; the scratches were that deep.

This experience didn't make me fear or dislike cats, but I do have a healthy respect for what they can do with their claws when they want to!

I grew up with all sorts of animals. Besides cats and dogs, we had birds and fish. I had a turtle named Terry the Turtle. I would put him on the piano bench beside me when I practiced and he would bob his head along with the music.

My brother Lou and I collected snakes and lizards. We found a place that would buy them from us: two cents for a garter snake and three cents for lizards. I wonder what the place did with them?

My father would bring home injured animals he found at construction sites. We had an owl he nursed back to health and an armadillo that I walked on a leash in the backyard. My father had an amazing way with animals. He would put the world's best animal communicator to shame. He understood animals and they understood and obeyed him.

He was old-school, though, and we ate our fair share of the animals we raised: chickens, rabbits, and turkeys. We also ate animals he and my brothers hunted or caught: frogs, wild rabbits, squirrels, fish, and even snakes.

We always had a vegetable garden and fruit trees. Frequently at dinnertime, we kids were sent outside to harvest the vegetables for dinner. String beans, squash, lettuce, tomatoes, carrots, cucumbers, we grew all of these and more. We had peach and pear trees, and grew our own figs. We even had a banana tree which, because of the weather, only produced small fruit once in awhile.

My father raised bees and I happily helped him care for them and harvest the honey. I had my own bee suit for protection and was only stung a few times, usually not while harvesting the honey but when playing too close to flowers. We always had jars and jars of honey for ourselves and to share with others. To this day, I love bees and find their ability to live as a community to be fascinating. And I love honey.

My dad had homing pigeons for awhile. It was fun to put some of them in his Jeep, drive them out to the country, and then release them. Who would get home first? Them or us? They did, of course!

Although there were some ways in which my family was dysfunctional (aren't they all?), I am very grateful that I was raised in a family that taught me love of nature as well as a healthy ability to be self-reliant. From a young age, I cooked, cleaned, did laundry, and contributed to the running of the household. I didn't get paid for doing this. We children lived there and were expected to contribute. Growing up as a girl with two brothers in the 1950s, I did more household chores than they did, while their chores tended to include more lawn mowing and car washing.

We didn't get allowances. When we got a little older, every once in awhile my father would stand at his dresser and make three piles of money; one for each of my brothers and a smaller one for me. He felt the boys should get more money than the girl should. Of course, this made me jealous of my brothers and gave me the hurdle to overcome of believing women should not earn as much as men.

This was part of his generational make-up. It is an attitude we still fight as a culture today.

We went to the country almost every weekend and camped out. We boated, fished, read books, and went swimming and waterskiing.

It got pretty hot in the summer in south Texas. We didn't have air conditioning. When it was really hot at night, we would all take our sheets and pillows outside in the backyard and sleep under the stars. We would look at the various planets and constellations and name them. My mother was very good at this since she taught science in school.

One of my favorite games as a child was playing schoolteacher. I lined-up my various dolls and stuffed toys and sat them so they could face a small blackboard. Pretending to be a teacher, I would hold class and write on the blackboard so my students could learn.

This was copying my mother, of course, but it also foreshadowed the role of teacher I would later play.

Don't we all remember posing for those annual yearbook photos? Did your photographer give you a free comb? Ours always did.

And throughout all of this, I prayed, went to Mass, and wanted to become a nun.

All my life I have had issues with my weight. From a young age, I was told I was fat and my mother put me on my first diet at the age of four. The few photos I have of myself at this age don't show a fat child at all. When we're told something enough times, though, we believe it and make it so.

In my adult years, I realized that my mother saw herself as fat and she wanted to save me from having to deal with being overweight.

My youth was spent on one diet or another and being deprived of the foods my brothers enjoyed. It's hard on a young body to be on a diet when it is trying to grow and develop. I remember being hungry most of the time.

One of the ways I dealt with this was to hide food when I could and eat it when no one was looking. As I grew older, I would go to the corner market and buy donuts, cookies, and soda and hide out by the dumpster to devour them before returning home.

Of course, I did begin to put on weight! Off to the doctor we went, where tests showed me to have an underactive thyroid gland. On to medication I went! By the time I was 14, I weighed 163 pounds. Some of the rude kids at school called me names and, of course, that hurt.

Children make fun of one another for lots of different reasons. There's something about our need to always have someone we consider "other." Parents don't realize how much they influence this in their children by speaking negatively in the home about other groups of people. It will be nice someday when we all see one another as people; as the brothers and sisters we truly are to one another.

· · · · ·

Rest Stop

Our childhood experiences give us the base upon which we build our adult lives. Have you ever thought about your childhood experiences and what they mean to you today? It can be very enlightening to write your autobiography, going into as much detail as you can.

This can be especially useful for people who are questioning their life's work, who wonder what direction they should take in their lives. Frequently, our childhood experiences reveal the path we need to take in order to fulfill ourselves.

What interests did you have? What were you good at? What sort of challenges did you have to overcome and how did you do it? Who were the most important people to you when you were growing up and what did they teach you about life and about yourself?

If you have unresolved issues from your childhood, what have you done about them? Living with unresolved childhood issues can be like trying to walk with a boat anchor around your neck. It might be scary to face your past, but it is scarier to face the future when these issues have not been resolved.

There are some wonderful counselors and therapists who are willing to support you in the exploration of unresolved childhood issues. Find one you can work with and use these issues to fuel your walk towards success and fulfillment on all levels of your being. One of the miracles of good therapy is being seen and accepted by one other person who doesn't judge you.

On the other hand, don't hide behind childhood issues or abuse and let them hold you captive. Some people define themselves by what happened to them in childhood. Therapy is meant to help you integrate and heal such experiences, not keep you in bondage to them. Get in, do your work, and move on. Don't become a career client.

Let's get back on the highway and move along....

I go to the convent.

As far back as I can remember, I wanted to be a Catholic nun. I'm sure one of the reasons was because I was raised around nuns, but I think it goes deeper than this. I think that when we have yearnings and talents that begin at a very young age, they are carry-overs from prior lifetimes. Whenever I see or hear about young children who show special talents or gifts, I always wonder who they were in a prior life.

Even as a child, I had a strong affinity for feeling the sacred in life and I enjoyed the ritual and trappings of Catholic Mass, chanting, praying and meditating. Clearly to me now, I had done all of this before.

Those of us who grow up Catholic are encouraged to find our vocation or calling in life. Some people, we were told, are called to be married, while others are called to living the religious life. Whenever I prayed about this, I always felt I was called to the religious life.

At the age of 15, I entered a Catholic convent. In those days, some orders of nuns accepted girls after they had completed the 8th grade. The order I joined wanted me to wait until I had finished two years of high school. Since I was always younger than my peers, I was 15 when I finished my sophomore year of high school.

I researched various orders of nuns and even went on a sleepover at one large convent where they allowed young girls to come and experience life in the convent in order to find out whether or not they had a vocation. That order wasn't for me. Instead, I chose a small Irish order. These nuns had been my teachers since 6th grade so they knew me well and I knew them. At the time I entered, the convent was home to only 24 nuns.

My mother was mostly supportive of my going to the convent, although she did ask me several times if I was sure this was what I wanted to do. I'm not certain how my father felt since we didn't talk about it. He was not a talkative man.

Years later after her death, I discovered my mother had been in the convent studying to become a nun and was forced to leave because her father was ill and she had to take care of him. How I wish she had told me this so we could have discussed it. I can only guess she was ashamed at having left but will never know for sure.

I was given a list of items to bring with me to the convent. These were personal care items such as soap, toothbrush and nail brush, as well as the clothing I was to wear. There was certain underwear I was to bring that had long legs that came mid-thigh. When they arrived in the mail, I looked them over and wondered how I could ever wear them and survive the Texas heat in the summertime. My mother made my dresses for me. The nuns provided my head covering.

When one first joins the convent, they spend a year as a postulant. Another young woman who was 16 entered at the same time I did, so we went through this training together. I will call her Susan.

Our first day in the convent was an exciting one. Both sets of families came to watch as, with much ceremony, we were accepted into the convent. Afterwards, our families enjoyed cookies and tea while everyone visited. Finally, the families left and Susan and I were officially living in the convent.

I will never forget that first night. Susan and I shared a room and had both prepared to go to bed. There are times when silence is observed in the convent and this was one of those times. The Great Silence is observed from 10 p.m. until after breakfast in the morning, so we didn't speak to one another. But we did look at each other with huge smiles; we were so incredibly happy to be in the convent where we could spend our time with God and living for God.

I remember that after Susan had crawled into her bed, I stood at the window and looked outside at the moon in the sky. I sighed a huge sigh and thought, "Finally, I am where I belong." I felt I had come home at last.

People ask me if I felt homesick. I was only 15 and this was the second time I was away from home without my parents or siblings, but honestly, no I didn't. I felt relief. This relief was partly because I was now out of a dysfunctional home environment, but mostly it was because I was once again in a spiritual community.

As I said earlier, I believe in reincarnation and I have a difficult time understanding why anyone would doubt that this is how the world is set up. Reincarnation just makes sense to me now.

I remember the first time I was introduced to the concept of reincarnation. I had no trouble accepting it right away. I think the reason I was so happy to be in the convent was because of other lifetimes I have lived in such settings. I believe I have lived in some sort of religious orders or ashrams in prior lifetimes.

· · · · ·

Rest Stop

If the concept of reincarnation is new to you, please don't dismiss it without some exploration, especially if you are of the Christian faith and rely on the Christian Bible. Reincarnation was taught as a matter of course in the early years of Christianity. The Church removed the teachings on reincarnation from the Bible in 451 A.D. This is a fascinating topic to research.

Lots of people refuse to believe in past lives because they can't remember them. Actually, it is a blessing that we don't remember our past lives. It is hard enough to try to remember everything that has happened in our current lifetime! Imagine if we were bombarded from memories of hundreds or thousands of lifetimes.

The value to being open to this concept is that when we are, it allows more of our talents and memories to come forward for use in our current lives.

Consider using your dreams to ask for information about prior lives. Sometimes useful information can be revealed this way. Or consider finding a reputable past life regressionist who could lead you through a process of accessing information from past lifetimes that could help you today.

More than anything, I urge you to be open to the idea of reincarnation. Some fun surprises could show up for you.

Let's move on.

Life in the convent.

People ask me what it was like living in the convent. I understand their curiosity, so let me explain how things worked in my convent in the 1960s. I can't speak about the daily routines of other orders, but I did have nuns from other orders as friends and much of this was the same for them. However, I am sure there were and are differences. I am speaking for my experience only.

The first year in the convent, one is called a postulant. We didn't wear the full nun gear but did have our own habit or dressing requirements. We wore long black dresses, a black cape, and a modified head gear which allowed the front of our hair to show. We didn't cut our hair this first year. In fact, it was customary to let one's hair grow longer so the sacrifice would be greater at the next stage when our hair was cut very short.

During our first year, Susan and I went to a local high school where we both finished our last two years in one year. It was an all-girls high school and we attended classes right along with the rest of the girls. We didn't participate in any of the after school activities or sports or go to the prom. We also didn't get printed high school diplomas or go to our graduation ceremony. But we did graduate.

This first year is somewhat of a boot camp for nuns. We weren't allowed to speak to the other nuns, who were called professed nuns and who had taken their vows of poverty, chastity, and obedience. The exception to this rule was special holidays such as Christmas when we were allowed to speak to them. There was a nun called the Mistress of Novices. She was in charge of us, our activities, and our spiritual practices and education.

She was very strict but had a good heart. I'll call her Mother Francis. It was her job to tell us what books to read as well as to be sure we said our rosaries and Office (nun's daily prayers based on the Psalms, said three times a day), meditated, and went to daily Mass.

Because we were in training to be real nuns, we had to practice the vows we would take someday: poverty, chastity, and obedience. Poverty meant we didn't own anything. Everything was owned by the community. We had no money and never went shopping! There were other longtime nuns who took care of the community food-buying, other purchases, and paying the bills.

At last I was where I wanted to be: a postulant in the convent where I could dedicate my life to God and spiritual service. I don't think convents accept 15-year-old girls anymore. That is quite a big life decision to make at such a young age. I was happy.

If we needed something like toothpaste, tissue or toilet paper, or shampoo, we had to go to Mother Francis' room or cell, as our rooms were called. She would leave her door open if she was in and available to us. A closed door meant she was out or didn't want to be disturbed.

When I knocked on her door, she would say "enter" or "yes." Usually she was sitting in a chair at her desk. I would then kneel beside her, put my hands under my cape, bow my head, and say, "Mother, may I please have (fill in the blank)." She would say, "Yes," and then we would both go to a closet in the hall where she took out whatever it was I had asked for and give it to me.

The closet was a fun place because it was kept fairly well-stocked. Many of the gifts we received went into this closet. If my family gave me something for my birthday or Christmas, I would take the gift to Mother

Francis, kneel beside her, and ask if I could keep it. Many times she said yes, but sometimes she didn't. Then the gift went into the general coffers for distribution to anyone.

This was to teach us to be non-attached to material things, which is what the vow of poverty is all about. The vow of poverty does not mean that nuns don't have anything, because they certainly do. Our needs, although simple, were well-met. But I didn't own anything. Everything belonged to the community and I was given what I needed when I needed it. And I understood anything could be taken from me at any time. I didn't own anything.

I didn't have much trouble with this. It seemed a little strange to kneel beside someone and ask for a tube of toothpaste, but I understood what I was doing and why. There were some other young nuns who had a lot more trouble than I did. One of them had entered when she was 18 and she was always questioning why she couldn't keep gifts her family gave her. She found this rule difficult and felt it was unfair.

The convent was maintained by everyone doing some of the work. Besides cleaning the shared rooms or cells and bathrooms, each of us was assigned certain rooms in the common areas. We would mop and dust daily and do deep cleaning several times a year. This is one of the reasons convents sparkle!

Postulants are given extra chores to do. We were usually given some of the more lowly and dirty tasks, such as taking out the trash cans.

Not only did Susan and I take out the trash cans to the street for pickup, it was also our job to wash the empty cans with soap and water, dry them out, and then line them with newspaper. If we didn't do this correctly or forgot to do it, we had to ask for penance.

Asking for penance was similar to asking for goods I needed. A knock on the door was followed by a "Come in" or "Yes." I knelt down and then proceeded to say, "Mother, I ask for penance because I (fill in the blank)." Mother Francis would then tell me why this was a bad thing to have done or not done and give me a certain number of Hail Marys or Our Fathers to say.

These prayers had to be said in the chapel while lying fully prostrate on my belly and chest, face on the floor, in front of the altar. Both Susan and I would wait as late at night as we could, hoping no one would see us saying our penance. Usually one or more nuns would be present. It was embarrassing. I always wanted to tell them what I had done so they wouldn't think I was really bad. But I couldn't talk to the other nuns anywhere and certainly not in the chapel.

One of the most frustrating reasons to ask for penance was because the sugar bowls or salt and pepper shakers were empty at the head table, the table where the Mother Superiors ate. After every meal, Susan and I would go to all the tables in the refectory (dining room) and be sure everyone's shakers and bowls were full.

When it came time for lunch and one of us was called to task because there was no sugar for the Mother Superiors' tea, we were very frustrated. One of us had just filled it after breakfast. How could it be empty by lunchtime?

The day I stopped being a postulant and became a novice meant wearing a wedding dress and enjoying wedding cake as I "married" Jesus. Two years later I would actually take my first vows.

Each of us had to ask for penance more than once before we figured out what was going on. When she ran out of sugar or salt while cooking, the cook, Sister James, would run and take some off the Superiors' table instead of getting her refill from the stock closet! The tables were closer and easier for her to use.

I have to admit that once we figured this out, we weren't very nun-like in our discussion about it. The problem was that we weren't allowed to speak with her so we couldn't confront her. We told Mother Francis about it but nothing was done. We had to start checking the sugar bowls and salt shakers before and after every meal.

During most meals, we didn't speak. We ate in silence. The nuns took turns reading aloud from a spiritual book at the beginning of the meal after we said grace together. As postulants, we took our turns reading as well. It was frightening at first. Here I was reading aloud to nuns who had taught me in school. Was I pronouncing the words correctly? Was I loud enough?

Over time, I got used to it.

The novitiate is a two-year process. The first year is called the spiritual year and is spent in silence, prayer, and meditation. A first-year novice is not allowed to leave the convent grounds or to have visitors, except at Christmas and her birthday. This is probably as difficult for most parents as it is for the novices.

Once the postulant year was over, Susan and I were ready to become novices. During our spiritual year we did a lot of spiritual reading, had classes with one of the older nuns, said the rosary a lot, and had several meditation periods daily instead of the usual two most of the nuns had.

Our spiritual year began with a ceremony where we were "married" to Jesus. We even wore wedding gowns. During the service, we layed prostrate on the floor, giving ourselves over to Christ. Midway during the ceremony, several nuns whisked us out of the chapel to an adjoining room where we removed the wedding gowns and put on the formal nun's habit. The only difference was that our headgear was white and everyone else's was black.

This is also the time where the scissors came out and the long hair we had been growing was chopped off. Yes, I said chopped. Whacked is more like what actually happened. A nun grabbed a handful of hair and chopped it off unevenly and in clumps.

Then we went back into the chapel with our nun outfits on, the ceremony was completed and there was a great celebration, including a big wedding cake.

Both of our families were there to celebrate with us. I have no idea what they thought of the goings-on. I was just so happy to have taken this next step. Now, I really looked like a nun and dressed like one.

That night in our room, Susan and I took turns trying

My father and mother visited me in the convent and posed for a photo in the middle of a field of blue bonnets behind the convent.

to even out our hair. It didn't really matter because no one but us would see it, but it felt better to have our hair neatly trimmed and there was less chance of our headgear falling off.

My spiritual year was one of the best years of my life. I didn't have to do anything but pray, meditate, do some physical labor and cleaning, and learn how to be a good nun. I loved it.

My days were spent in the chapel praying, walking the grounds saying the rosary, sitting in meditation, studying religious literature, with some time being spent cleaning the convent inside and out.

There were also situations set up to teach us obedience. One time the Mistress of Novices told us to remove all the rocks on one side of the pathway that ran between the buildings to the other side of the pathway. This took us a few days.

When we were finished with the task, we told her we were done. She told us to move the rocks back to where they had been before. We were not allowed to ask why or to complain about this. Being obedient meant we did as she said. I will admit, however, that we did give one another silent looks that adequately expressed our frustration with having to do such backbreaking work for no apparent good reason.

We were allowed an hour of recreation daily. This usually meant sitting with some other novices and chatting while doing embroidery or darning our stockings. We repaired as many of our clothes as we could rather than throwing them out. This was part of the vow of poverty and is a practice society could use more. I still have difficulty throwing things away if they can be used by someone.

We didn't watch television or listen to music as a general rule. There were, however, exceptions.

When President Kennedy was assassinated, all of us were allowed to gather around the television and watch the funeral. It was a sad time and impacted all of us deeply.

When the Beatles were on the Ed Sullivan Show, we were also allowed to watch. Because the Beatles were from England and most of the nuns were from Ireland, they felt a kinship with the performers and wanted to see what their singing was like.

Part of the beauty of the spiritual year is that the novices are given the luxury of not having to work outside the convent, to be unconcerned about material needs or goals, and to have the opportunity to focus on their spiritual lives. Who would want to do this at the age of 16? I did. And it is a memory I will carry with me the rest of my life.

The second year as a novice, this spiritual paradise was over: I started college. I went to a woman's college that was run by another order of nuns. I wanted to study psychology. My superiors wanted me to study piano pedagogy. Here is where the vow of obedience comes in.

This order didn't need a psychologist. But the nun who had been the main music teacher was getting ready to retire so they did need someone with a degree in music. And that was supposed to be me.

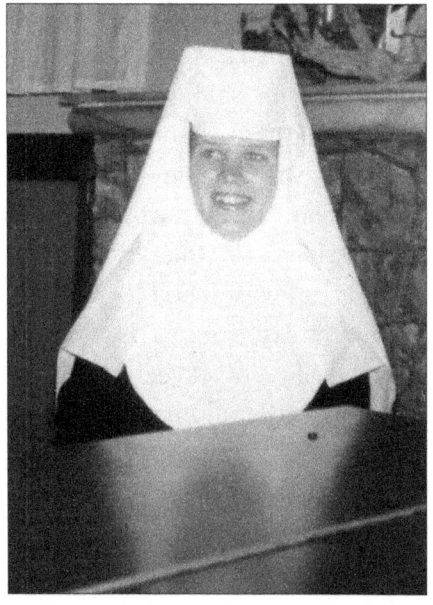

During my spiritual year in the novitiate, I was in heaven. I prayed, meditated, said the rosary, read spiritual books, and did some physical labor. Yes, that headgear got pretty hot in the Texas summer heat!

Although I had asked to study psychology, I was told no. Having been raised in a musical family, it made sense for me to study music. So I did.

My mother was an accomplished pianist and organist. She also played cello when she was younger. When I was a child, not only was I raised on classical music but I also started playing the piano at the age of four. Every morning before I left for school, I practiced the piano at least a half hour and then another half hour in the evening. My brother Lou had the same schedule and sometimes we played duets together.

In the convent we did have a record player in the recreation room. While studying music in college, one time I had to write a term paper about some aspect of contemporary music. Somehow I had learned of Simon and Garfunkel and decided to write my paper about their music.

I brought one of their albums home with me from college and took it to the recreation room to play it and make notes for my term paper. One of the very stern nuns happened to come into the room while the record was playing. She stormed over to the record player, removed the needle, and demanded to know why I was listening to profane music.

I explained I was working on a term paper for school. She was highly indignant and said she was reporting me to the Mistress of Novices who would take care of punishing me. Then she stormed out again.

After she left, I put the music back on and finished what I was doing. I never heard another word about this incident. Fortunately, I had requested permission to use the record player so when the nun reported me she found out I wasn't doing anything wrong. Did she ever apologize? No.

Every day, three of us took a car and drove to the college where we all studied different subjects. I was friends with other students in my classes. Since it was a Catholic college, I was given a lot of respect for being a nun. I also had a lot of fun with my fellow students.

A typical day looked like this. Up at 5 a.m. Meditation and prayers at 5:30 am. Mass at 6:30 am. Breakfast at 7 am. Cleaned the rooms I was responsible for. Off to school by 8 am. When I got home, I had more prayers to say, then practiced the piano and did my homework. Dinner was at 6 pm. Usually, there was an hour of recreation after dinner.

At 9 pm, we said our evening prayers in the chapel. The Great Silence began after night prayers and didn't end until after breakfast the next morning. It was called the Great Silence because there had to be a huge reason to speak. During other times of silence, one could whisper if something needed to be said.

The purpose of observing silence so much was to allow us to stay centered within and practice the presence of God. Generally, I had no trouble with keeping silence although once in awhile something funny would happen and it was difficult not to laugh.

After my second year of being a novice, it was time for me to become a professed nun and take my first temporary vows. This meant they lasted for a year. After a week's retreat where we prayed and fasted in silence, there was a ceremony where we took our vows and had a reception afterwards.

This is when I also received a big rosary that hung from my belt. If you were around nuns in these days, I'm sure you remember the big rosaries nuns wore. Postulants and novices didn't wear big rosaries. It was a huge deal to get your rosary and Susan and I were happy. Of course, we were called Sister by then.

I continued going to school and I continued to love my life as a nun. I thought I had found my true place in life and I planned to be a nun for the rest of my life.

It was close to the end of this year that things started to go sour for me. I began to have terrible headaches for no apparent reason. And I began to doubt that I should be a nun. Honestly, I can't tell you how this happened and over the years I have forgotten many of the detailed thoughts and feelings I had.

The headaches were so bad, there was many a night when I didn't sleep. By this time I had a cell to myself and it was right beside the neighbor's house. This was in an area that had been out in the country and right next to my window was an old windmill that squeaked, turned and whined all night long.

In the Texas summers, the weather got very hot and we didn't have air conditioning so my window needed to be open. Combine one headache with an annoying windmill and one gets a night of no sleep.

As nuns, we each had a spiritual director who was a priest. We would meet with him once every few months, discuss our spiritual life and practices, and ask for advice or prayers if we wanted to. I began to talk to my director about my doubts that I should be in the convent.

I can't remember everything he said to me, but at first he encouraged me to hunker down, continue being a good nun, and trust that this was some sort of test for me to pass. After awhile, though, he began to say that perhaps I should consider leaving the convent.

I was heartbroken. Here I was being a good nun, living my dream, and it was clearly not working out for me. I prayed about it and discussed it with one of the nuns who had become my friend. I also spoke with my Mother Superior who was a woman I deeply admired.

It was summertime and one of the parishioners had lent the nuns their cottage by the ocean. We spent a week there relaxing, praying, reading and swimming in the ocean. Yes, we wore one-piece swimsuits with t-shirts underneath for modesty's sake.

One night after everyone had gone to sleep, I walked down to the pier that reached out into the ocean. It was a full moon and the beauty of the moon shining on the water almost took my breath away.

I remember talking to God and asking what I should do. What was His will for me? Should I stay in the convent or should I leave? I was afraid of the answer because I didn't want to leave and go out into the world. I was only 19 years old, soon to be 20. I remember listening to the sounds of the waves, smelling the thick salt air, and hearing unmistakably that I should leave. My time in the convent was over and it was time for me to go out into the world; for what purpose I didn't know. I was sad but I was also glad that my path had been made clear at last.

When I returned home to the convent, I sought out the Mother Superior and told her what had happened. We both saw the signs were clear that I needed to leave. Because I had made my temporary vows for the second time only a few months prior to this decision, I had to write to the local bishop for dispensation from my vows. Had I taken my permanent vows, I would have had to write to the Pope for dispensation.

People ask if I could have left without permission. Yes, I could have done that if I didn't care about staying a member of the Catholic Church. At that point, I wanted to stay in the Church and wanted to play by the rules.

And this is where it turned ugly.

·····

Rest Stop

What is your spiritual history? Think back to your childhood, teen years, and early adulthood. What were your beliefs? Did you belong to a church? Were your parents religious? How have your religious beliefs changed over the years? Are you agnostic or atheist? How do you think this history influences your decisions and choices of today?

There's no right or wrong to this. Your past is only that: your past. However, it can and does inform the present. Some of your spiritual attitudes can be traced to your earlier life as well as to other lifetimes.

Spending some time exploring this can help you see yourself more clearly and can be very helpful in living life the way you choose today.

Let's hop aboard and continue.

Leaving the convent.

Yes, ugly. Very ugly. Once word spread in the convent that I was asking for dispensation from my vows and was leaving the convent, it was as if I had come down with leprosy. No one would talk to me except the Mother Superior and the nun who had become my friend. If I ran into any of the nuns outside on the walkway, they would actually step off the walkway and avert their eyes while I walked past.

Words cannot express the depth of heartbreak and devastation I felt. These women had been my family for the past five years and I had known some of them since childhood. We had shared a home, our vocations, laughter, and tears. Now, because I was leaving, they would have nothing to do with me. I find it impossible to express how betrayed I felt. These many years later, I still remember the pain my younger self felt.

After taking my vows of poverty, chastity, and obedience, I was a full-fledged nun and incredibly happy. I had no idea that 10 months after this photo was taken, I would leave the convent and begin a totally new life.

People have asked me why I didn't confront the nuns and try to make them talk to me, to ask them to explain what they were doing. Remember, I had lived the last five years within a very strict structure. There was obedience, times of silence, people I could and could not talk to. I was low woman on the totem pole. I washed trash cans. People who know me today can't see me as the timid and obedient 19-year-old I was.

Confrontation never entered my mind. These women were holier than I was. They were closer to God than I was. They knew more than I did. If I was being treated this way, in my heart of hearts I believed I deserved it.

After having spent my teenage years in a convent, I was going out into the world. Although I didn't want to do it, I called my mother who was not very happy with me, but she did take me shopping. I was able to get two dresses, some shoes, and underwear.

The situation became so difficult for me that one Friday I decided to leave without permission from the Bishop. I couldn't take the rejection any longer. I started to walk to the Mother Superior's room when I ran into her on the sidewalk and she said the letter had come. I could leave the next morning.

She told me to call my mother to come and get me and that I should leave during Mass without saying goodbye to anyone. My last night in the convent was a long and lonely one. I didn't know what my future held. I knew I was doing the right thing and didn't understand why I felt so awful.

I prayed for some comfort and for some sign that I was doing the right thing. Nothing came. Even God had deserted me.

The next morning, my mother showed up. I was in one of my two new dresses and had the other one in a paper bag along with my college books and music. I had to leave my prayer books and rosary and nun clothes, of course. Feeling rejected and full of shame for my decision, I got into the car and we drove away.

The day I left the convent, my dear mother wanted me to dye my hair red to match hers. I declined.

One of the first things my mother said to me was this. "I would like for you to dye your hair red like mine so none of my friends will know this isn't my natural color."

I was back into the world I had known before going into the convent, but I promised myself I wouldn't stay there long. I told my mother I would think about it, but had no intentions of turning my hair red to match hers.

My new life had begun.

Life after the convent.

On Friday, I had attended my classes at college in my habit or nun-suit. On Monday, I showed up in one of my new dresses with very short, uneven, hair. Because no one at college knew I was thinking of leaving the convent, at first my fellow students didn't recognize me. It didn't take long, though.

I was mortified because I looked pretty bad. Not only was my hair a mess, but I was overweight, didn't know how to wear makeup, had only the two dresses, and still acted like a nun. People still treated me like a nun. They didn't know how to act around me and I didn't know how not to be a nun.

I knew I had to find a part-time job quickly and I knew I had to leave my parents' house as soon as I could before my mother tried to make me over in her image. Much as I loved my mother, I realized that if I stayed living in her house it wouldn't be long before she and I would have some serious misunderstandings. The best course of action was to find my own way in the world as quickly as I could.

During all of this my dad didn't say much to me at all. He was not unkind, in fact, he let me use an old car so I could drive myself to school. I had gotten my driver's license while in the convent.

Because I was studying music at the time, I played both the piano and the organ and sang. I began to look for a job as a church organist. Catholic churches didn't pay their organists or choir directors, so I had to look to the Protestant churches for a job.

I found one. A small rural Lutheran church hired me to be their organist and choir director for $98 a month. Yes, you read that correctly, a month.

Meanwhile, I began hiring myself out as a piano teacher and built-up my teaching roster with students while I also played the organ for weddings and funerals. I was able to cobble enough money together to support myself.

Once out of the convent, I had kept in touch with the one nun who was my friend. Through her, I found a widow who wanted to rent out a room for $50 a month.

It wasn't long before I had moved out of my parent's home and was going to college on my own, supporting myself with my music. It still amazes me that I found the strength and skills to do this. It never occurred to me to look for a regular job or to leave college. The natural thing for me was to use my skills and creativity to support myself, and it worked. This attitude of relying on my own talents and creativity has served me well over the years.

It was during this period that I left the Catholic church. I decided that I didn't want to belong to a church that preached love and practiced the exact opposite.

A priest I had known my entire life died a few months after I left the convent. He had baptized me when I was an infant, and he was always part of my life because he lived in the neighborhood where I grew up and where the convent was located. I went to the church where his body was laid out, and as I stood looking at him, I thanked him for all he had meant to me in my life. Then I said, "Father, I know this will disappoint you, but I am leaving the church. The way I was treated when I left the convent is inexcusable, and I can't believe this is what Jesus taught or how he meant us to treat one another. I think you will understand. Goodbye to you and goodbye to the Catholic church." I left and didn't return to a Catholic church until my father died many years later.

I decided I was agnostic. I did believe in God but I wasn't sure what or who God was. I just knew he wasn't the God of my childhood or of the nuns.

I decided that God was an alien who lived on another planet and this is the God I would pray to. He/She/It was a God of love. And this was my God for the next 15 years.

Rest Stop

In order to continue with our lives, sometimes we have to make a big move. Sometimes we have to break ties with people or situations. Is there someone or something you need to let go of or move away from in order to grow?

This can be difficult, yes, but if it is the right move for you, you will find the inner strength and the outer support you need.

The first step is to make the decision that it is time for you to move on. Once you have done that, give yourself the gift of a pause to ask for guidance about how to make the move. Meditate, pray, journal, and write down what you hear.

Then come up with a plan of action. Come up with your plan of support. Write it all down. Set dates for when various aspects of your plan will take place.

Get your tools together. Will you need certain books, audio programs, classes, support groups? Friends? Counselor? Minister? Healer? Line it all up. Set a date for the big move. Then jump. Do it. Trust that the universe will support you because it will.

Call on God as you see Him/Her/It to help you. Who is God to you? If you have been damaged by religion or religious groups, you might have to do as I did and decide your own definition of God. There's nothing wrong with that. God is very flexible and loves us even when we think we are totally unlovable.

Decide. Pray. Plan. Jump. Trust.

Moving right along now....

Washing the nun out of me.

College life went on. I became more secure in my civilian life, made new friends, and threw myself into becoming an ex-nun. This is when I learned how to smoke cigarettes, drink alcohol, dance, wear makeup, grow my hair long, and go along with the crowd. This was tough to do at a Catholic women's college, but bit-by-bit, I managed.

My fellow students stopped seeing me as a nun and began to invite me to parties. I joined the college choir. Did they know how to party! I got jobs playing the piano for school plays so became part of the theater crowd. They also knew how to party. I met some of the most imaginative and creative people in the drama and music departments of college.

I began to date. My first date was with a fellow musician and we went to a symphony concert together, followed by a visit to the local donut shop. I moved out of the widow's home into an old house with a roommate, and continued my work as piano teacher and choir director. I also kept a good relationship with my mom and went to some musical events with her. She eventually forgave me for not dying my hair red to match hers.

Some Sunday mornings were really tough. After a late night of partying – or shall we say early morning of partying – it was tough to show up at the Sunday service and lead my Lutheran choir. But I did it. Amazing what youthful energy can pull off.

But the nun was still not washed out of me. I kept running into people who knew me as a nun and expected me to act like one. I even ran into some of my former sisters from the convent. Something needed to happen for me to truly live my life without what I saw as the nun-baggage. I became seriously depressed at one point and even considered suicide.

My roommate took a lot of prescription drugs and I knew where she kept them. One night while she was on a date with her boyfriend, I took out the pills and sat on the floor listening to a Moody Blues album and contemplated taking enough drugs to end my life. Fortunately, self-preservation kicked in and I realized I needed a new environment. I knew that as long as I stayed where I was, I would not be able to grow into whoever it was I needed to become.

So, while taking my last few college courses and practicing for my end-of-the-year piano concerto with the college orchestra, I quit college and moved 200 miles away where no one knew me.

I took a few days off, drove to the big city of Houston, went to an employment agency and interviewed for a job as receptionist at an oil company. I only typed 40-words a minute but that was enough. The following Monday, the agency called me and said I got the job.

After finding teachers for my piano students and giving notice at the church, I packed everything I owned into my red VW Bug and hit the road to my new life. The convent was two years behind me, and my life was wide open before me.

· · · · ·

Rest Stop

Sometimes we have to reinvent ourselves in order to move forward. What are you trying to do in your life right now? Do you need to become a different person, learn new skills, acquire new attitudes, behave differently? What within you needs to change for this to happen? Can you let go of the way things are, of who you think you are, so you can move forward toward your goals?

If so, use the same ideas from the last time we rested.

Decide. Pray. Plan. Jump. Trust.

The puppy chapter.

Perhaps you remember when Ellen Degeneres had her first television show, a sitcom. In the fourth season, 1997, there was an episode where the character she played made an announcement: "I'm gay." Because the producers didn't want the public to get wind of the show until it aired, it was called "The Puppy Episode."

This is my Puppy Chapter. Yes, I am gay. The reason I'm mentioning it this early in the book is because being gay is part and parcel of who I am. Trying to tell my story without talking about my gayness means leaving out part of who I am. And it is only part of who I am. Being gay is about so much more than sexual expression. It's about who we love in an intimate, committed relationship. It's about who we want to join as life partners.

Just as is true for heterosexual folks, gay couples' lives revolve around the day-to-day tasks of living, not just what does or doesn't happen behind bedroom doors.

Sexuality is an interesting topic, though, especially when it comes to religion and spirituality. Some religious teachings encourage people not to have sex unless they are married and want to have children. Sex, they say, is only for procreation; nothing else.

Other teachings say sexuality is part of human nature and it is meant to be enjoyed whether or not one wants to have children.

Some teachings frown severely on homosexuality, while others say God doesn't care at all. Some of the people who are against it say it isn't natural, that gay people choose to be gay, that God didn't create gay people.

A minister I know likes to explain it this way: we don't choose our sexuality. We discover our sexuality. When he talks to people who are anti-gay because they believe gay people choose to be this way and can change into heterosexuals any time they want to, he says this:

Think back to when you were young and were just beginning to notice the opposite sex and the feelings you had when you were around them. Remember as you reached puberty, how your body began to respond to people and images of people of the opposite sex.

Now ask yourself: did you choose for this to happen? Or did it simply happen and then you learned what it meant?

It's no different, he explains, for gay people. The only difference is gay people have these feelings for people of the same sex rather than for people of the opposite sex. We don't choose to be gay any more than you choose to be non-gay.

The big difference is that heterosexual people receive positive feedback and support for their feelings. Gay people are told that what we feel is wrong, we are bad and sinful, and we shouldn't talk about these feelings and certainly shouldn't act on them.

Gay people have to come to terms with and accept who we are and this is frequently a long and difficult path with many side roads. Adolescence is a difficult time for everyone and even more so for people outside the accepted social sexual norm.

Generally, gay people don't have much support for the process we go through although this has been changing and continues to change as society matures and learns to accept everyone for who they are.

Many gay children are thrown out of their homes for being gay or sent to a program where someone tries to force them to become heterosexual.

If you are heterosexual, imagine being 15 or 16 years old and not only being told you're bad and sinful but your parents taking you to a place where you are locked up and shown people of the opposite sex while being given electric shocks. Or you're preached at 24/7 until you agree you are a sinner for having thoughts and feelings about the opposite sex and then agree to have a gay relationship and even marry someone of the same sex. Then and only then will you be considered healed.

This happens to gay children and it can take years for them to be themselves if they ever do.

Without knowing the word for it, I knew I was gay when I was around

11 or 12 years old. This was when my girlfriends at school began making comments about boys as well as when they began to pay more attention to their appearance, wanting to wear makeup, etc.

I remember wondering what the fuss was all about. The words we heard when I was growing up were: homosexual, queer, dyke, and fag. And I knew being that was wrong.

One day when I was in the convent, there was a phone call for me. When I answered it, there was a young man on the phone who told me he had something awful to tell me. He said my brother Lou was a fag, a queer, and that he was violent. I didn't know what to say. I was shocked that someone I didn't even know would call and tell me this.

I confided the nature of the call to my close nun-friend and we agreed to keep this to ourselves and to pray for both of them.

One day after I had left the convent, my brother called me and said he had something to tell me. He wanted to come by and take me out for a drink so we could talk. I said okay and he came over to my apartment. We got in his car and he drove us to a bar.

When we walked into the bar, I looked around and, except for me, there were only men there. We sat at a table and he ordered beers for us. Then he said, "Do you know what I want tell you?"

"Yes," I said, "This is a queer bar and you want to tell me you're queer."

"Yes," he said, "but we don't use that word. We call ourselves gay. Queer is a negative term."

We spent the evening with my brother telling me about his coming out process and I told him about the phone call I had received in the convent. He said that man was a former boyfriend and he had threatened to tell our entire family. I told my brother that I loved him and that his being gay didn't make a difference in how I felt about him.

Not long after this conversation, we decided to rent a two-bedroom apartment together. I was still going to college and he was working in a music store.

I still had not come to terms with my sexuality although I did question it. I just figured I was heterosexual and buried any feelings or thoughts to the contrary. Many of my new friends were involved in sexual relationships, some of them even having affairs with married men. I thought it was time for me to take the plunge. This was, I knew, one of the best ways to get that nun out of me, big-time!

One of my friends had four brothers and the oldest one had been flirting heavily with me. He was several years older and quite worldly compared to the rest of us, with his own apartment and job. I decided that he would be my first. My brother helped me plan for the event.

We decided to have a birthday party for me, invite some friends over, including this man. Then once the party got going and we all had had enough to drink, I would take this fellow upstairs to my room and see what happened. I did and it did.

I have to say I wasn't very impressed, but that didn't keep me from trying again and again. It became fairly apparent to me that people made a big deal out of something that I found to be a pretty average experience. That is, until I realized I was doing it with the wrong people.

As with many gay people, my coming-out process was long and involved and it took me many years before I was able to accept this part of myself. I've written on this subject several times and many people have found my articles on this topic quite helpful.

Do you feel the way I do? I'm getting soul-weary hearing about the bullying going on, about the gay/lesbian/bisexual/transgendered (GLBT) students who are committing suicide because they are being bullied by their peers. Yes, and it makes me angry. It has to stop.

I like to think that I live in a civilized society but lately I have started to wonder. A lot of people blame the children who are being bullies and I agree that they must be held accountable, both legally and morally. I also think it has to go much farther than that.

Where do children learn to be bullies? Where do children learn to disrespect people who are different than they are? Where do children learn to be homophobic or racist or woman-hating?

Two places. Number one, in the home from their parents and other relatives. Number two, from the larger society around them.

I see a lot of bullying going on in the larger culture. Groups yelling at one another, trying to push each other around, telling lies about each other, and generally showing little to no respect for one another. Children see this and what do you think it teaches them?

We see a group of consenting adults having their rights to be married being voted on by the rest of the population, and denied in some areas of the country. What are children to think about that? Of course they think GLBT children have something wrong with them, otherwise the adults would vote to give them their rights, wouldn't they?

Church groups that claim to follow the teachings of Jesus Christ are among the worst offenders when it comes to discriminating against GLBT people. If Jesus hadn't ascended, he would be turning in his grave to hear what is being said in his name.

Even in what should be more enlightened spiritual circles, there's a lingering attitude of discrimination against GLBT people, that somehow we are not quite as capable of spiritual growth as our heterosexual siblings.

If we want the bullying of GLBT children to stop, all of us must be willing to stand up for everyone's rights. We must be willing to stand our ground and demand that all human beings are respected, whether or not we understand them, whether or not we are afraid of them.

In the GLBT community, there is a well-known saying: "Better blatant than latent." People are always shocked when they learn that a minister who is violently anti-gay is exposed as someone having secret gay love affairs. I'm never shocked by that. The more violently someone pushes against gay people, the clearer it is that he or she has unresolved sexual orientation issues of their own.

People who are comfortable with their sexual orientation don't feel the need to persecute, control, or diminish GLBT people.

And what about the GLBT children and the self-hatred that causes them to agree with their attackers and kill themselves? They have absorbed the messages being sent to them even before they knew their orientation.

If you're on a spiritual path, I suspect you believe that at the level of soul there is no male or female. We're beings who incarnate here as one or the other because we want to have certain experiences. If you believe this, then why would it matter to you whether two beings in male-suits or two beings in female-suits are drawn to a life together?

Don't you think this has more to do with their individual soul paths and very little to do with you or anyone else? Rather than pushing such people away, wouldn't it be a better idea to find out more about how they tick? How they think and feel?

If you believe in reincarnation, isn't it possible that you could come back as a gay person someday? Wouldn't you want to come back to a world that accepts you rather than one that pushes you away and punishes you for being who you are? Which world do you want to be part of now? Even on a selfish level, I would think you would prefer a world without discrimination.

If you agree with me that it is time for us to have a just and fair society for all people, then start speaking up whenever you can. If you have children or are around children, be sure they know how you feel and help them grow up as loving and accepting people. If you're around bullies of any age, don't tolerate it. Speak up and help them learn to be accepting of all people. Isn't that what you want for yourself?

· · · · ·

Rest Stop

Whatever your sexual orientation or gender identification, are you comfortable with yourself? Sexuality runs the gamut from people who choose to be celibate to those who are in committed relationships to those who are experimenting with their sexuality. Each of these is appropriate for the different people involved as long as they honor themselves and others and are in relationships with other consenting adults.

Our sexuality is only one part of who we are. Are you happy with your current sexual expression? If not, would you be willing to work with a therapist or minister who could help you?

Are you comfortable with the sexual expression of your adult children, parents, neighbors, friends? Do you realize this doesn't have anything to do with you? Could you let go of judging others and allow them the same freedom of expression you would like to have?

If this is a charged issue for you, breathe into it, relax, and ask for higher guidance as to the best next step for yourself.

Let's move on.

Learning about life.

The next 13 years were full ones. I decided I wanted to pursue my original idea for a college degree in psychology. I signed up for night school and worked fulltime while attending college and studying in the evenings, making sure I still had time for some fun.

I thought it would be a grand idea if I could work in the field of psychology while studying it in school and found out about a job as receptionist at a drug treatment clinic.

When I interviewed for the job, I suggested to the supervisor that if he hired me, it would be a great idea to promote me as I learned more and got my degree. He agreed, gave me the job, and kept his promise to promote me.

First, I became an intake interviewer. This meant I met and interviewed each new client and their family who came for treatment.

Ah, at last, the nun was washed out of me! Long hair: check. Blonde: check. Partying: check. Smoking and drinking: check. The inner nun was subdued, at least for awhile. No one would ever guess this woman had been a nun.

What a fabulous way to learn about family systems and the path many drug addicts take to their addiction. This gave me an inside look at people and their early life experiences. It also helped me gain an understanding of what parents go through when children don't turn out the way the parents want them to.

It was wonderful to learn how to see situations from various points of view. The parents saw one situation while the child who turned to drugs saw it differently. Both viewpoints were valid.

It was amazing to me how people would open to a total stranger and share some pretty dark secrets. Later I realized my being a stranger who didn't judge them helped people to be more open. The more I learned about people and what shaped them into being who they were, the more open and accepting I became of all people. This laid a wonderful groundwork for me to be able to encourage people to open up to me quickly in any setting as well as teaching me to be accepting of everyone.

When you see inside people's hearts and life experiences, you learn we're all essentially the same. We're here to have different life experiences, yes, but we're all the same.

Once I had my degree, I was promoted to Counselor and I had my own caseload. I worked mostly with teens and young adults who had issues with what we called soft drugs. Over time, however, the clinic changed and we started seeing more hardcore addicts and we opened a Methadone clinic. Methadone is a drug that reduces withdrawl symptoms in people addicted to heroin or other narcotic drugs without giving them the high they experience with the street drug.

This was my introduction to heroin addicts and people on probation and parole. I found this more challenging and interesting and ended up moving to a different job at another drug clinic. This one specialized in working with the hardcore drug addicts. Everyone on my

Although I went through a phase of doing my best to be "butch," it never really suited me. This look, however, did help some of my drug clients to take me a little more seriously.

caseload was either on probation or had just come out of prison and was on parole.

This was yet another chance to see a different part of life. I had to learn how to be very strong, use curse words, yell at people, and deal with criminals.

I learned my lessons well and could keep up with the best – or worst – of them. As a counselor at this particular treatment program, you either learned how to enforce rules and codes of conduct or the clients would have their way by manipulating you. Some of my fellow counselors were former drug addicts and they were very helpful in teaching me how to tell when someone was manipulating or running a game on me.

After about a year, I received a promotion. I was to be the lead counselor at one of the clinic's outreach centers. This one was located in one of the primarily black areas of town. Not only was I white, but I had long blonde hair and drove a white MG midget. My staff consisted of two Black counselors, one Latino ex-addict counselor, and a Black receptionist. Our caseloads were racially mixed.

To this day, I can't imagine why I was promoted to this position. But being a young and brash woman in her mid-20s, I accepted it. Another book would be required for all the stories I could tell so I will just share a few of them here.

"We're going to rape you!"

One day I was alone in the clinic when four men walked in and said they were going to rape me. They stood between me and the door that led outside. I had had a similar situation with a client the prior year: a very tall, muscular, convicted rapist and drug addict who was out of prison on parole. One of the conditions of his parole was that he had to have counseling sessions twice a week. If he missed sessions, used drugs, or got arrested for anything, he would have to go back to prison.

During one session, he stood over me and threatened to rape me. I had bluffed my way out of that situation by standing up and getting very close to his face and saying, "Fine. I dare you to rape me because you know what? I'll hurt for a little while but you'll hurt for a long time. You rape me and you go back to jail for at least ten years. Make your choice."

We had a stare-down. I kept looking him in the eye as best I could. He was 6'4" and I was 5'6" so it meant looking up at him. He backed down and left the room in anger. I got him transferred to someone else's caseload. So, I thought, that worked once before. Maybe I could bluff my way out of this one, too.

What was on my side was the fact that I could smell alcohol on the men. I could tell they were sauced-up so I figured their reflexes were probably pretty slow. If I could just get past them, the door wasn't far away and I would be outside where there were other people.

I gathered my energies up, threw my shoulders back, and started walking with great force and purpose right towards them while laughing and saying loudly, "Sure, you're going to rape me. With as much liquor as you've had, I doubt any of you could even get it up much less know what to do with it."

They were so startled at this reaction that I was able to push my way between them and out the door. I stood there holding the door open and sternly told them to get out and never come back. I was out on the sidewalk by the street now as the clinic was a redesigned storefront. There were people walking by who noticed what was going on and stopped to watch.

"Come on," I yelled sternly. "Get the f___ out of there right now and never come back!"

They stumbled out, growled at me as they walked past, and took off down the street. I ran back inside, locked the door, and called my supervisor to tell him what had happened.

He was a former police officer and had helped me learn how to be tough. He laughed and said he would have loved to see their faces when I pulled that off and congratulated me.

Whose urine?

Our clients had to give us urine specimens two to three times a week in order to prove they were not using drugs. A specimen that tested "dirty" (positive for drugs) could send some of them back to jail. The male counselors had to witness the male clients giving their specimen and the female counselors had to witness the women.

We usually knew ahead of time whose urine would test positive by the way people behaved and how their eyes appeared. One time there was a fellow we all suspected of using drugs. We expected his urine to come back positive for drugs but it kept coming back from the lab negative.

I told the male counselors to pay close attention to how he gave his urine specimen because I knew he was pulling this off somehow. One time we had a woman who manipulated the process by hiding a small jar inside herself. It was covered with plastic wrap and contained someone else's urine. When she went to give her specimen, she broke the plastic and out came the clean urine. I suspected this fellow was doing something similar.

Eventually, we discovered he had a hot water bottle with someone else's urine in it. The hot water bottle was under him arm. He had a tube running from the hot water bottle down his side and under his penis. When he appeared to be giving his specimen, he pushed the hot water bottle with his arm and out the urine flowed into the specimen bottle. It appeared he was actually urinating. And the bottle felt warm to the touch because he had the fake specimen close to his body.

Once the male counselor caught him, the young man was so proud of himself. I told him, "If you would spend even a fraction of your time channeling your creativity in positive, legal directions you could do something with your life." Instead, he went back to prison.

Dr. Jack

Another time, I was at the home office turning in some reports. I had just walked out into the reception area. Walking in the front door in handcuffs and accompanied by two police officers was one of the psychiatrists I had worked with at my former drug treatment clinic.

I looked at him. He looked at me. We both blinked. I said, "Dr. Jack, what are you doing here and why are you wearing handcuffs?"

"I got arrested for selling prescriptions to clients at the other treatment center and instead of going to prison, I have to attend the inpatient program here."

He was clearly embarrassed. I remembered how nervous he always was at the other clinic and how often he would be late for his appointments. The pieces fell into place.

I asked him, "Were you using drugs at the other clinic?"

"Yes," he said. "I was."

I wished him luck while realizing no one is immune to addiction or greed.

Padding his paycheck

This next story ended up being one of the reasons I left the drug counseling field. Besides being a thankless job with a terrible recidivism rate, it didn't pay very well.

I noticed that one of my newer counselors who was also an ex-addict and ex-convict, seemed to have a lot of money. I also noticed that he spent a lot of time with his female clients. I began to suspect he was running a hooker service out of the clinic using his clients.

One day I decided to confront him. Right after one of his clients had left, I went into his office and caught him with a roll of bills in his hand.

"You're running hookers, aren't you? You're using our clients as hookers!"

He smiled at me slowly and chuckled.

"I was wondering when you would figure it out. Yes. How could anyone live on what they pay us? But you will never prove it. I will deny it. And because of the equal employment laws, they will never fire me."

He was right. My bosses wouldn't do anything about it. I decided it was time for me to move on. I made a lot less money supervising a drug clinic while maintaining my own caseload of 24 people than did most of my clients. They had to show me their pay stubs every week to prove they were working so I knew they made over twice what I did.

What kind of jobs did many of them have? They worked in machine shops. I decided that's what I wanted to do. Let the drug addicts work out their own addictions. I was going to go cut iron and make some money.

· · · · ·

Rest Stop

There are many types of addictions from things like sugar and cigarettes all the way to hard core drugs. But, there are other types of addictions: addictions to ways of thinking and judging other people, food, the internet, pornography, television, etc.

Are you addicted to something? Are you willing to think about letting it go? There are lots of programs that can help you, but you have to take the first step of being willing to change.

Lots of times we aren't willing to change until we become so uncomfortable that we are forced to. It's smart not to wait that long. Addictions are insidious and can be soul-destroying. If you have a substance abuse problem, be brave, reach out for help, and do something about it.

Although I tried marijuana twice in my 20s, I didn't try other illegal drugs. I think the reason is because I saw firsthand the damage drugs did to the people I counseled. However, I did enjoy alcohol to excess and I was deeply addicted to cigarettes for many years. Here's the story of how I finally quit smoking. Perhaps it will inspire you.

Kicking the habit!

After 20 years of being a dedicated, devout cigarette smoker, I released the habit March 25, 1989. Many people want to know how I did it.

I started smoking at the age of 21 for two very specific reasons. I had been out of the convent for a year and was having trouble with my weight, an ongoing issue as you know, since the age of four. I decided to use cigarettes when I was hungry instead of eating. I also was having difficulty with other people and myself accepting that I was no longer a nun. I decided to begin engaging in un-nunlike behaviors to help everyone understand I was not a Sister anymore. Smoking was one of those behaviors. Cigarettes helped enormously with both issues and became a friend for me.

As with other smokers, cigarettes became a part of my life, part of my identity. They comforted me, accepted me unconditionally, were always there for me when I needed them, gave me pleasure and a feeling of security. I never thought about giving them up until 1983 when I became involved in a fitness program and experienced shortness of breath when doing aerobics or swimming.

Over the next few years, I tried several programs: hypnotherapy, aversive conditioning, prayer, programming crystals, and good old willpower, all to no avail.

What I knew to be true was, and is, that we give up our addictions when they no longer serve us and not a second sooner. I have frequently said this to others and have even written about it. I now know this to be true with every cell of my being and offer it as solace to others who are struggling with an addiction. When we are ready to give up our addictions, we will be drawn to the right method for us. But it isn't the method which accomplishes the task, it is our readiness.

Despite that knowledge, I continued to beat myself up and make myself wrong for smoking cigarettes. Especially within New Age spiritual circles, one is inclined to feel very not-okay if one smokes. I remember being in a New Age bookstore one day and having a woman walk up to me and say, "Do you mean to tell me you still smoke cigarettes? I gave them up and I see so much clearer now. You really should stop smoking."

This was in front of several other people. Mirror or not, I looked her in the eye and said, "What I do is my business. I'll quit smoking when I am good and ready and not a minute before."

There was another time I was at a spiritual gathering and went outside to have a cigarette. I was followed outside and given a lecture about how bad it was for me to smoke and about how offensive it was to others. So, why follow me and my smoke outside?

When I had started therapy as part of my spiritual path three years before quitting smoking, it was one of the issues on my agenda as was letting go of alcohol. My therapist asked her clients to make a contract not to use alcohol during the course of therapy so I had to let go of it right away. I agreed with her that one can't go deeply into emotional issues while still under the influence of drugs, alcohol, marijuana, etc. But she didn't demand that I give up my cigarettes. Good thing, too. She would have had one less client.

During the course of therapy, I would bring up the issue of cigarettes and my inability to quit. I tried several times again, unsuccessfully. Three hours was tops for me to go without a smoke! We're talking a major addiction.

During this time, I was also faced with the uncomfortable decision to print articles in the newspaper I owned, The New Times (more on this in a later chapter), articles which were insulting to smokers. I cringed as I saw the articles go into print and only hoped my fellow smokers would not take the information inside themselves and feel even more guilty about their habit.

I hoped they would remember we all have our addictions; smokers' just show and have become the focus of a lot of judgment by other people. Many folks not addicted to substances are very addicted to thoughts and mindsets such as judging others!

One day during a therapy session when I had "become" my inner child, "she" was crying and feeling very desperate about my attempts to quit smoking. She said that, to her, cigarettes represented the unconditional parenting love she never received as a child. In the context of the emotional healing work I was doing at the time, I understood completely.

My therapist, being very wise, had the adult me promise my child-self that I would not quit smoking until she told me she was ready to do so. I made that promise and I kept it. I continued working on my issues, allowed myself my addiction and became less judgmental of myself despite what the world around me said about smoking. At least I was consciously addicted, knew what I was accomplishing through the addiction, and was using it rather than it using me.

About a year later, I began to feel that maybe, just maybe, all of me was ready to let go of cigarettes. My partner gave me a beautiful cigarette lighter for Christmas and my first thought was, "What will I do with this if I quit smoking this year?" Not long after, I began to feel the strong desire to release cigarettes.

One Saturday, I asked my Higher Self for guidance that could help me quit smoking. I had read *How to Quit Smoking* by Herbert Brean – an outstanding book. I was getting ready to choose a date to quit and knew that I needed to make preparations for my journey because that is how I saw what I was doing. This was a journey into myself, a journey of self-discovery. The idea came to make a journey bag.

For me as for many others, part of being addicted to cigarettes was the manual part of it: holding the cigarette, lighting it, fiddling with the pack before opening it or taking a cigarette out of it. To succeed, I knew I would need something to replace all of this manual activity. I made my journey bag and began filling it with my new non-smoking paraphernalia!

Besides my *How to Quit Smoking* book, into the journey bag went a smaller bag with seashells I could hold and rattle together, a very comforting sound for me; shards of obsidian to ground my energy (something smoking used to do for me); chewing gum and mints; and an amethyst wand about four inches long that was to serve as my cigarette when I felt the need to hold something.

Part of smoking for me was the smoke. I loved the smoke. What could I replace this with? Incense, of course! And I realized I could use my beautiful lighter to light my incense. Smoking while I drove used to be very important for me. What was I going to do while I drove to and from work every day? I got an incense holder which fit on my dashboard so I could burn incense. Sometimes I would also hold a stick of incense while driving to have the feel of the cigarette.

It was fun to see other drivers' reactions when in bumper to bumper traffic and they would see the incense burning on my dashboard. Into the bag went a variety of incense.

I had chosen my quit date. It was two weeks away and I was still making preparations emotionally and physically. I was saying good bye to an old friend who had served and comforted me well. One Saturday, I asked my inner child to draw a picture of how she was feeling about my decision to quit. The picture showed a child sitting on top of a tall pole, vulnerable, exposed to the whole world and not safe at all. I decided to meditate and asked for guidance to comfort my inner child, to find out how to give her what she needed without the cigarettes.

In the meditation, my higher self became a small child and talked with my inner child. She explained to the child that she was totally safe now and had several people to care for her, mostly me as an adult. I don't remember the rest of the conversation, but when it was over an inner voice said, "If you want to quit smoking now, you can do it."

I was in disbelief. My quit date was still two weeks away. Could I give up two whole weeks of still smoking? Did I want to do that? I felt as if I had been infused with a tremendous strength and ability to let go of cigarettes. I decided not to risk losing it since sometimes moments like that don't return rapidly. I have not smoked since.

Although the first few days were very difficult physically since I cold-turkeyed without anything to help me with the withdrawal, I was amazed at how easy it was overall. I lived with a smoker and had wondered how that would affect me. There were very few times that being around cigarettes affected me. It was rare that I even thought of having a cigarette and eventually stopped feeling deprived without them. I didn't feel in agony like I had the other times I tried to stop.

I don't hate cigarettes or their smoke. Although some will judge me for this statement, I honor what cigarettes did for me. I honor them as a friend who moved away, a friend I don't see anymore but towards whom I still hold affectionate feelings. I am grateful to my addiction for the comfort, warmth and support it provided to me. And I am grateful that I no longer need this friend.

Why did I quit if I feel so positive towards cigarettes? Didn't I quit because of the hacking coughs, the expense, etc.? No. The reason I wanted to quit was because I didn't like being addicted to a physical substance. I didn't like the fact that I no longer chose whether to smoke or not to smoke; I had to smoke. I was addicted. This is why I quit. I wanted my freedom of choice back.

And I have that. I took back my freedom and it feels very good. More importantly, the part of me who needed the cigarettes to feel okay doesn't need them any more. I feel wonderful without them, something I never thought I would be able to say. In fact, after quitting there were times when I would comfort myself with the fact that I no longer smoked. When taking a deep clear breath I thought, "No one can take this away from me. This feeling of freedom, this feeling of deep satisfaction with who I am and with my life, no one can take it away from me. I can give it up if I choose to do so, but it belongs to me and no one can take it away."

And what did I learn? If we have an addiction, there is a reason for it. We are not bad people; we are not weak-willed; we are not stupid or inconsiderate of those around us. We have a deep emotional need that is being met by the addiction. If we want to let go of the addiction, we must find another way to meet our needs. I think we have to give up addictions such as alcohol, cocaine, marijuana, or other mind-altering substances in order to deal with the issues underlying them. (Not all healers agree with me on this.) I believe these addictions mask our feelings to such an extent that clarity is very difficult while still using them.

With cigarettes and perhaps other addictions such as food, sugar, television, and the internet, it may be possible, even necessary, to continue the addiction while we work on the needs being met through them.

Our addictions are places we can grow, areas within us which need our love, not our condemnation. They remain with us as long as we need them to without judgment. Some addictions might stay for an entire lifetime. I believe many of us have addictions just so we can learn unconditional self-love. And if someday we decide we no longer need our addictions, it is important to know we can let them go.

God/dess loves us whether we smoke, do drugs, carouse, gamble, or watch every midday soap opera. Maybe other folks withdraw their affection or understanding from us because of behaviors we engage in, but God/dess doesn't. We continue to evolve through our addictions, even when we are unaware of how we're evolving.

We can and do walk our spiritual paths even when addicted to something; so, if you are addicted to something, please don't let anyone tell you otherwise or make you feel "less than" because of your addiction.

You are not a hypocrite; you are not a sinner; you are not deserving of being labeled a social outcast. Each of us is God/dess expressing through us as us, no matter what we do or don't do. That fact can't be changed by anyone.

Now, let's get back on the road and see where I landed next!

Women don't cut iron— or do they?

The local newspaper had an ad for machinist trainees. This is what my clients were doing and making a ton of money so why shouldn't I?

When I showed up to apply, I was told that women didn't do this kind of work. Besides, I had a college degree. Why would I want to get my hands dirty and maybe hurt myself?

Because I wanted to make money, that's why. Besides, laws had been recently passed that said it was illegal to discriminate against women. This was the early 1970s.

I told the human resources manager that I would make him a deal. Let me take the aptitude test. If I passed it, he should hire me. If I didn't pass, fine. I would leave.

Remember earlier when I said I was grateful to my dad for letting me help him fix his cars and work with the carpentry projects? Yes, I aced the aptitude tests.

Reluctantly, the human resources manager said he would let me interview with the shop foreman. "But," he said, "You won't be hired. Our foreman doesn't want women working with machines in the shop."

The shop foreman was a tall, lanky fellow who was in his 50s. I could see he had been around the block a few times and was very sure of himself. We walked around the shop and he showed me the different machines where men were at work. He said he couldn't understand why I would want to get dirty or hurt myself by cutting iron.

We walked past a table where three women were sitting. I asked what they were doing. He said, "This is where women belong in machine shops. They inspect the parts that the men make. It is safe and they get to sit all day."

I asked if they made the same money as the men did. "Of course not," he smiled at me. "It's easier work so why would we pay them the same amount of money?"

We ended our tour on a catwalk high above the machines running in the shop below. It was hot, noisy, and smelled bad. He said, "So, we do have an opening for an inspector trainee. How about that job?"

"No," I said. "I want the job advertised for a machinist trainee and I'll make you a deal. You show me one machine in this shop that it takes a penis to run and I will walk out of here and never come back. If you can't do that, hire me and see how I do."

His face turned red, he gritted his teeth and snarled at me, "Ok, girlie. You're hired. Trust me, you won't last 30 days. Get your gear and be here tomorrow morning at 7 a.m. sharp!"

The next morning I showed up with my safety glasses and steel-toed boots and two years of working in machine shops began! The first few weeks were terrible. The first day, the foreman put me on a machine that was called the screw machine. Seriously, that's what it was called.

The machine spewed hot pieces of iron shavings and nasty, oily coolant at me. When I was done that first day, I looked like some sort of creature that had been caught in a disaster. And I smelled awful from the nasty coolant. My back and feet, arms and legs hurt like they never had before. But I came back the next day and the next.

The guys in the shop began to respect me because I didn't ask for favors and I worked hard. Some of them used drugs or were on probation or parole and I loved that I didn't have to do anything about it.

I found out that the general manager who was a short, elderly man would stand in the back of the shop with his hands in his pockets watching me work, rolling back and forth on his heels, smiling and telling the foreman, "Hire more women!"

We worked eight to twelve hours a day, three weeks in a row, including weekends. The shop was closed down one weekend a month and all of us had two days off. Everyone did this except the office staff. People who objected to the schedule didn't last. I didn't care for it and it was grueling. I didn't have time for anything but work. I was also making good money because we were paid time-and-a-half on Saturdays and double-time on Sundays and holidays.

Raises kept coming at increments of ten cents an hour and I learned how to operate and repair more machines. Eventually, I was trained to operate the newest and most expensive machine in the shop, what's called a Numerical Control or NC lathe machine. These were the first computerized lathes and it was an honor to be trained to operate and repair them.

And this is how I met a serial killer named Gary Taylor.

• • • • •

Rest Stop

Here's a question for you. Do you let other people define you? Do you let other people or society tell you what you can and can't do? Are there things you really want to do but don't because someone would criticize you?

If you can say yes to any of these, it's time for you to take a break and find out why. Why are the opinions of other people more important to you than your own happiness? This is your life. No one can live it but you. When you are dying, do you want to have regrets about not being who you really wanted to be?

Terry Cole-Whittaker wrote a book called, *What You Think of Me is None of My Business*. I have always said she didn't have to write the book because the title says it all. Other people's thoughts and opinions don't matter unless you chose to let them.

Get in touch with your inner self, find out who you are meant to be. Then go and be and do what your soul is calling you to be and do. It might surprise you that the very people who judged you the harshest will become your best supporters. They will respect you for being true to yourself.

Give it a try and see what happens!

Now let's go meet that serial killer, shall we?

How I met a serial killer and lived to talk about it.

All kinds of people work in machine shops. Some are just regular folks making a living. Others are true artisans at their work. Others use drugs and are on probation and parole. And then there's Gary.

I operated one of the new NC machines on the swing shift, 3:30 to midnight. Gary ran the other NC machine on the night shift. He would come in early and stand around talking to me. At first, I was nice to him because I thought he was just another one of the guys. Then he started hurling insults at me for no reason and calling me a feminazi, among other things.

He came up with some pretty outlandish statements, things that didn't always make a lot of sense. I started to try to ignore him because he got so riled-up. Trying to have an actual conversation with him was not possible. When he spoke to me, his eyes got wild and he had a wicked smile. It was frightening.

One day I was asked to work a double shift. This would mean I had to work right beside Gary for the entire night. But I told the boss, sure, I would work the double shift.

What a horrible night it was. All night long Gary hurled hateful insults at me. I ignored him but he continued. I told my supervisor and asked if he would please tell Gary to stop talking to me. The supervisor said to work it out myself and walked away.

When the shift finally ended, I got my things and went to punch out on the time clock. Gary was right behind me. He spoke in a sweet, kind voice, and said he was really sorry for everything he had said to me and wanted to take me to breakfast.

I wanted to make peace with the guy but everything in me said not to go.

As I drove home that morning, I felt like someone was following me but once I was at home I didn't see anyone behind me. I thought it could be Gary but didn't see him anywhere so put him out of my mind.

I had bought a larger toolbox for my work and was trying to sell my smaller one. Gary decided he wanted it so I sold it to him. We had a few more words at various times, but nothing like the night we had to work together.

A few weeks passed and I didn't see Gary for awhile. I figured he was on vacation. One afternoon I came in to work and there were police cars in the parking lot. When I got to my machine, the foreman told me not to start work. He said the police wanted to talk to me. I asked, "Why?" He said, "It's about Gary. They've talked to most of us already."

I was led into one of the offices and there was a male and a female detective sitting behind the desk. They looked at me; then at each other, and told me to have a seat.

There had been a series of 16 rapes and murders in the city and they told me they thought Gary was the one responsible for them. He was in custody, but there was a chance he could get out. They said I matched the physical type of woman he enjoyed killing. They also told me he had committed murders in other cities and had been wrongly released from a prison for the criminally insane. He had been on the lam for awhile, hiding in plain site at our machine shop.

They asked me about the arguments Gary and I had and wanted details about that and about the toolbox I had sold him. I told them about the various arguments we would have and about his inviting me out for breakfast to make up.

They showed me some polaroid photos of some of the bodies of the victims. They were women who had been beaten, killed, and then wrapped in black plastic bags held in place by chains. It was a terrible thing to see and I am sure my face went pale. This was before the days of television and movies where every type of violence is shown graphically. I had never seen anything like this and was horrified.

I asked why they were showing me these photos. The male officer said, "We want you to be scared. He could get out and if he does he will come after you. We believe the only reason he didn't kill you was because he knew that would draw the police here and we would find him. Now that we've found him, if he gets out, he will come after you. He has nothing to lose. Here's my card. If anything happens call me."

"From the grave?" I thought to myself. The police said they were sorry they couldn't do more, but that they would call me right away if Gary was released from jail.

The next few weeks were difficult ones for me. My skin crawled as I felt someone behind me almost all the time. My next door neighbor in the apartment complex where I lived was a Texas Highway Patrol officer. Our paths rarely met, but I knocked on his door, told him what was going on, and said if I banged on our adjoining walls for him to call 911 right away and then to come over to my apartment with his gun drawn! He looked at me as if he wasn't sure I was telling the truth, but said he would call 911 if he heard anything suspicious.

I looked into getting a trained attack dog but couldn't afford one. I had never felt this sort of fear before. My friends were all supportive, to a degree. No one offered to let me stay with them or to come and stay with me! I guess they didn't want to be a potential victim, either.

Gary was extradited because he was wanted in Washington state. He had killed many people and ended up in prison where he still is today. The crime writer Ann Rule devotes a chapter to him in her book *You Belong to Me and Other True Crime Cases* where the details of his crimes can be found.

I tell this story when I give classes on getting in touch with and following inner guidance. Everything in me said not to go to breakfast with Gary that morning, even though he was being nice to me. I am sure if I had gone to breakfast with him, he would have killed me. This is a pretty drastic way to learn to pay attention to your feelings and follow them and it is a lesson I have never forgotten.

It also shows that we die when it is our time and not before.

Another machine shop

Not long after this, I went to work at a different machine shop. Although I had heard a rumor I was going to be promoted to second shift foreman, I wanted to work days. At this new shop, some of the men poured bourbon in their morning coffee. I thought this was a very dangerous practice for people who were working around machinery.

I worked on a computerized lathe there. This company had an on-staff programmer and he told me he was leaving the company before he told the bosses. He felt I would be perfect for the job so I took a course in programming and he helped me learn how to program the machine. I was the only person in the shop who could fix the machine and now I was learning how to program it, too. This saved the company a lot of money since they didn't have to call a repair man every time the machine quit working.

When it became known the programmer was leaving, I told the boss I wanted to be considered for the job. The programmer who was leaving told them I was qualified and would make a good programmer.

One day at the end of my shift, after others had left for the day, the boss came over to me and said, "I know you want this job as programmer. And I know you are qualified for the job. But I am not giving it to you. Do you know why? Because you're a woman. I don't care what the law says, I will do what I want. And you can't do anything about it because there are no witnesses to this conversation. I will never promote you." He smiled a big smile and walked away.

I was stunned speechless. I knew there was a lot of discrimination in the world but this was so blatant I couldn't believe what I was hearing. My machine was not running. It was down and I was repairing it. Remember I said I was the only one in the shop who knew how to fix it?

I did something I had never done before and haven't done since. After I saw the boss drive off, I packed up my tools, put them in my car and left never to return. I didn't even go back for my paycheck.

I am sure they got the machine running again but I also know it cost them a lot to get it repaired.

Gullible's Trabbles.

This period of time was one of meeting a lot of people and having a ton of experiences, some happy and others not. Just like life for everyone. There came a point when I said that if I was in a room of people and there were any nut cases there, I would meet them. It is as if I were a magnet for people who wanted to take advantage of me. I said that when I wrote my autobiography someday, I would call it *Gullible's Trabbles*.

To be fair to myself, I was an emotional teenager running around living as a grown-up. I had to be a grown-up because I had to work and support myself and try to make something of my life. But I was also trying to play catch-up with life itself. Some of the emotional skills people learn in high school I was learning in my early twenties.

Because they are interesting, I will share a few choice situations that came up for me.

One time a friend at college told me she knew of a garage apartment I could rent for a reasonable price. It was a single living area with an adjoining bathroom. The attraction for me was that it had a baby grand piano in it. At the time, I was spending eight hours a day practicing: four hours at the piano and four hours at a huge pipe organ at the college. To be able to practice some of the piano in my own home was a very attractive idea.

I went and looked at the apartment. It was in a remodeled garage behind a beautiful home where the owners, a married couple, lived. It was in a safe and upscale area of town. The owners liked me and I liked them so I rented the apartment. Everything was great for awhile. Then I started hearing some strange noises coming from the ceiling where the living area and the bathroom joined up. I wondered if there were some type of animals living in the other part of the garage. I began to feel the place was really creepy.

One day I decided to investigate. What did I find but the owner had drilled a hole in the ceiling and he was able to see everywhere in my apartment and bathroom. I decided not to say anything and just get out of there as quickly as I could. I moved some things around where the owner sat and watched me so he would know I was aware of what he was doing. When we saw each other, I just gave him a knowing look.

Then there was the parolee I knew who was 20 years older than I. He was a tall man with long hair, a full beard and a weathered face. He always looked very severe and wore a workman's jumpsuit. He was intimidating to look at but was really quite a teddy bear, I thought. I had met him when I was doing some outreach work meeting with some kids who used drugs but who weren't ready to come to our clinic for help.

We would met at a Denny's, drink coffee, and talk about their lives. When I didn't want more than friendship, he stalked me. He followed me everywhere and at night he was outside my home at all hours. I never considered calling the police because I didn't think he would hurt me. I also knew he would go back to prison. He didn't take action against me, eventually gave up and moved on.

This next one is actually funny now that it is in the past but it wasn't funny at the time. I was between jobs and had a job interview. I was properly attired for an interview in a business-appropriate dress. It was pouring rain. When I went out to the carport at my apartment complex, I discovered my MG Midget had no doors. During the night someone had stolen my doors. Really? Can you imagine the shock on my face when I realized my car had no doors? I thought I was dreaming. Unfortunately, I wasn't.

I couldn't cancel the appointment because I needed the job, so had to drive to the interview and try to keep the water in the road from splashing on to me too badly. MGs are very close to the ground so this was quite the challenge. When I called the insurance company I found out this was a common practice because these doors are quite expensive.

The insurance company paid for new doors and then cancelled my policy. I got a bright red Chevy Nova shortly after that and no one ever stole my car doors again.

Here's another great story. I took Spanish while attending night classes in college. We each had to have meetings with the professor in his office. When I met with him, he flirted heavily and let it be known he wanted a lot more from me. When I resisted and physically pulled away from him when he tried to kiss me, he got angry and said he would fail me unless I had sex with him. I didn't give in and he stayed angry with me but he did give me a passing grade. It never entered my mind to go to the administration and complain. The words sexual harrassment weren't well-known then, at least not to me.

• • • • •

Rest Stop

I don't know about you, but pulling off to the side of the road feels like a good idea right about now. The drug counseling and machine shop days were pretty intense years and I think they helped me do a good job of washing the nun out, at least for the time being!

Where was my spirituality during all of this? Yes, I prayed. Every evening I did pray to my God who lived on another planet. I always asked for blessings and healing for my family and others I knew. I think my prayers were answered. I also think my angels worked overtime keeping me safe.

Some people might look at these years of my life as being those of an ungrounded, lost soul who was looking for her right place. Although I can understand that viewpoint, I think it goes much deeper than that.

Throughout all of these experiences, there was a thread pulling and pushing me. Although I certainly could not have expressed it at the time, I do believe that my soul-self was behind all of this. I think it was the plan all along for me to meet all the people I met and have all the relationships I did.

It feels like I was finishing up karma with each of these people and when it was done, I moved on to the next experience. Because of these experiences, there are very few people I can't relate to or understand on some level. And I learned that everyone has a story. Everyone is here for a reason even if they don't know what the reason is.

Every person I met has enriched my life. Those who took advantage of my innocence – the landlord who drilled a hole in the ceiling of my apartment and was a peeping Tom; the Spanish teacher in college who wouldn't pass me unless I slept with him; the male friend who wouldn't take no for an answer and stalked me; the married man who raped me when I said I wanted to explore relationships with women; each of them helped to make me who I am today and I am thankful for the lessons they gave me.

During this time, I also met some wonderful people from whom I learned a lot. Because I was studying and working in the field of psychology, I learned a great deal about human nature and how the mind and emotions work. I learned a lot through the clients I met who faced their challenges with bravery and who did succeed in turning their lives around.

This taught me a lot about the human spirit as well as about the virtues of willpower, determination, foresight, and willingness to do the hard work of facing one's inner demons.

I was privileged to work with some fabulous psychologists and psychiatrists who truly cared about their clients, each other, and me as well as the rest of the staff. Love of all kinds does heal.

Do you know why you're here? Do you know why you have had and do have the relationships you do? If not, give yourself the gift of thinking back to everyone you've known and ask what was their gift to you and yours to them.

Did you complete each relationship? Sometimes we run away from relationships because they are painful and difficult. The challenge with that is if we don't complete the energetic exchange with that person, we will run into the energy again and again until we learn whatever the lesson is. If not in this lifetime, then in another.

Embrace your lessons willingly and you can move on much more quickly. No, I didn't consciously have this insight at the time and I suspect I could avoided some of these experiences if my understanding had been better. However, the stories do make for a great book!

Let's get back on the road, shall we?

Bouncing around and finding my place.

The next few years, I had quite a few jobs. I didn't want to go back to counseling drug addicts and also didn't want to go back to school to get my masters degree in psychology. I worked a number of jobs, including insurance sales, cosmetic consultant, a few days as a management trainee at 7-11, and a week or so in an employment agency. I quit that job when the boss said I had to discriminate against Blacks and Latinos by coding the applications. That way the company would never send minorities to employers who didn't want to hire them. Having worked closely with both Blacks and Latinos as well as having been discriminated against myself, I told them where they could put the job, and left.

I got a great job with a reputable employment agency and made a good career for myself as an employment consultant. I could use my psychological experience and know-how and also make a good living. Eventually, I moved into the higher echelon of the employment world by working with a head-hunting agency.

Headhunters are employment consultants who are hired to find people not actively looking for a new job and recruit them away from their current employer to work for the headhunter's client. This work involves some surreptitious skills such as ruse-calling, and at the time it paid very well.

Ruse-calling involves calling a company and using a pretense or ruse to get the names and positions of people in the company who might be appropriate for a job you're trying to fill. I specialized in placing accountants. Here's a ruse I used quite successfully:

I would call a company that I suspected employed the sort of accountant I was looking for. I would tell the receptionist that I was trying to reach one of their accountants I had met the previous day or evening. I would say I couldn't remember his name but he was about 25 or 26 years old (or whatever age I chose), and worked in the accounting department.

Invariably, the receptionist would start giving me names. "Was it John Dodd?" "No, I would say, I don't think so. What does he do there?"

She would proceed to tell me what the person did. We would keep this up until I got enough names and positions out of her. If I felt her getting suspicious, I would end the call saying maybe I had called the wrong company.

Then I waited a few days and called back asking for one of the people whose name I had gotten. Once they were on the line, I would tell them who I was and that a friend had told me they might be interested in a different job. I would get their home phone number and call them that night, interview them, and see if they fit the job I was recruiting for.

Of course, this wasn't a very honest thing to do but in recruiting all was considered fair. I got pretty good at this and enjoyed the challenge of the hunt.

I get married

Through a friend, I met my husband-to-be, and got married. Wait, didn't I say earlier that I am gay? Yes, I did.

It was not and is not uncommon for gay people to have heterosexual relationships and even to get married and have children. In fact, some gay people live their entire lives this way without ever being honest with themselves or their spouse. It is too difficult for them to imagine living marginalized by society. It is safer, they think, to pretend they are not gay.

What I find very sad is when someone who knows he (or she) is gay, gets married, and then has secret lovers or even goes to places like parks where he knows he can have anonymous sex with other men. I have heard numerous stories from gay men about some of the supposedly straight men, including men of the cloth, they have met this way.

As society becomes more accepting of gay people, it is my fond hope that fewer gay people will walk this route.

Although by this time I had had several gay relationships with women,

I was not out at all. I was very closeted and hid the truth of who I was from everyone, including myself. I went through phases of calling myself gay or bisexual.

I didn't and don't hate men. One of the things I had always heard about lesbians is that they are "man-haters." This only caused more confusion for me and, I suspect, for other gay men and women.

We don't hate the opposite sex at all. Just as heterosexual men and women don't hate other men and women just because they have intimate relationships with people of the opposite sex, we gay people don't hate people of the opposite sex just because our intimate relationships are with folks of the same sex.

Because I didn't hate men and, in fact, had had some good relationships with men, I questioned my sexual orientation for many years.

Although I didn't get married in a conscious attempt to hide who I was, at that time I would never have considered being open. I was definitely in the closet.

When Dan (not his real name) asked me to marry him, the voice inside my head said, "No!" But my mouth said, "Yes."

When we got married, Dan promised we would never leave Texas. Six months later, he said we were moving because of his job. I had a decision to make. Stay married to him and move to Canada or divorce him. I decided to move.

When this photo was taken, little did I know that the near future included a relocation to Vancouver, Canada, a move I fought and which ended up being my ticket to reawakening to my spirituality.

I didn't want to move and was sure I would be unhappy in my new life. That was a self-fulfilling prophecy. I was miserable in one of the most beautiful places on earth! I got a job at an employment agency there and made some new friends. But I wasn't happy. And I made sure he was as miserable as I was by complaining and refusing to enjoy anything.

One day when I was riding the bus home and looking out the window, I had the thought, "This is sure a beautiful place to live." I realized I had come to love the area and was actually beginning to be happy.

Through a series of events, I ended up buying the employment agency where I worked. This meant taking out a $40,000 second mortgage on our home. I knew the agency had issues but because I worked there and had experience in the industry, I knew I could solve the problems.

What I didn't know was that the world was headed for a serious recession. It was the early 1980s. When I bought the employment agency, there were 50 or more agencies in the area. Now there were 16 and I could no longer hold on and had to shut the doors.

This was a difficult time for me. I felt like a huge failure, was embarrassed, and felt badly about the debt I had saddled us with. I did, however, learn a lot about business through this experience and many of the things I did to try to hold on were solid business ideas I have been able to use and share with others since then.

One idea I had and implemented was to approach our local newspaper and offer to write a series of articles about how to find a job. Because so many people were out of work, they loved the idea and I had my first newspaper column. Perhaps this was a hint of things to come without my realizing it?

This is one of the ideas I give my business clients today: write articles for your local newspaper. They love the content and the exposure can be great for your business. Even with the internet and blogging, this tip still works for some businesses.

Dan loved playing golf so I learned to play golf as well. I wasn't very good at it, but I did enjoy walking the golf courses we played as well as the camaraderie that developed with other players. I had met a few women players over the past several years of playing golf. Once I wasn't working during the week while trying to find new employment, they invited me to play with them.

During one of these games, I met my new friend, Marsha.

Unbeknownst to either of us at the time, Marsha was to play an enormous role in my life.

The Reawakening.

During one of our golf games, Marsha and I were standing off to the side waiting for someone else to hit their ball when she asked, "Do you believe in psychics?"

"Hmm," I responded. "I don't believe or disbelieve. I haven't had much experience with psychics, so I don't know what to think about them. Why?"

"I have some friends who are psychics and they give psychic parties," Marsha explained. "It's sorta like a Tupperware party. You invite your friends over, they get readings from the psychics and then you get your readings free for hosting the party. I thought you might like to give a psychic party."

I thought about it for a minute and said, "Sure, why not! It sounds like something different and, who knows, maybe I'll get an idea of what I'm to do with the rest of my life!"

So began my reawakening to my spiritual life. I held the party and had several friends over. One of the psychics read tarot cards and sat with people at my dining room table. The other one had people go into our guest room. I didn't really understand what she did – until it was my turn.

I walked into the room for my reading, shut the door, and sat in a chair. The psychic closed her eyes, took a few deep breaths, and then began speaking in a strange voice that didn't sound like her at all. Later, I was to learn she was doing something called channeling. A disembodied spirit – a dead person – was speaking through her.

"All the keys have been turned and you are now ready to move forward in your life," she said.

That statement touched something deep within me and I knew it was true. I didn't really know what it meant; only that it was true. After she had finished my reading, she suggested that I get in touch with a local doctor she knew. She said I was under so much stress that this doctor could help me.

She explained that instead of going into a regular examination room, he had a darkened room with a recliner chair and a cassette player. He led his patients through a special relaxation session that he recorded. Then he had them listen to the tape daily.

I figured it couldn't hurt me, gave him a call, and made an appointment for the next week.

Sure enough, the session went exactly the way she had described. He said he was teaching me to meditate. It was different from what we had learned in the convent. After he had me relax and had said some very positive and interesting statements, he left the room and the music kept playing. I immediately had a spontaneous age regression where I saw all sorts of things about my life and myself beginning at the age of four.

When he came back into the room, he gave me the tape and said I was to listen to it every morning. In fact, on the tape he mimicked a popular commercial at the time: "Meditation is like the American Express card: never leave home without it." I did this exactly as he said I should and I kept a daily journal of my experiences. I had all sorts of visions and experiences that I would come to understand over the following couple of years.

Some of the ideas he put onto the tape were: "I never allow myself to think or say anything I don't want to see realized in my life;" and "If I find myself thinking a negative thought, I immediately say to myself, 'Cancel, cancel. Love, love.'"

This doctor also told me about a church he attended and he felt I would enjoy it as well. It was the Science of Mind church founded by Ernest Holmes. Today these churches are called the Centers for Spiritual Living.

Thus began my foray into the world of metaphysics and, eventually, my new career.

I started attending the Science of Mind Church every Sunday and took their entry level class on Wednesday evenings. I meditated daily and I began to practice what I was learning.

I immersed myself in the writings of Ernest Holmes, Joel Goldsmith, Eric Butterworth, John Randolf Price and his wife Jan, Donald Curtis, Catherine Ponder, and other New Thought writers.

I was also very drawn to Paramhansa Yogananda and carried his book *Metaphysical Meditations* with me and read from it frequently. I dove into the Bhagavad Gita, The Gospel of Sri Ramakrishna and became very interested in the then-living Indian saint Sai Baba.

I met some people from India who were followers of Sai Baba and they invited me to their home for chanting and meditation. I began going there regularly and received some *vibhuti*, sacred ash the saint was known to manifest. I learned that a person could write to Sai Baba and he would know of their requests and help them spiritually. I wrote to him more than once and felt he responded on an unseen level.

This was an amazing time of discovery for me and I absorbed as much as I could in a short amount of time.

I learned about manifesting, visualizing, and using affirmations. When I first learned about affirmations I got frustrated. People would give me an affirmation for this and another one for that. Before I knew it, I had 10 different affirmations going on. How was I supposed to focus on anything? I figured there had to be one affirmation I could use that would cover everything. I asked a teacher about this but he said he didn't know about such an affirmation.

When I saw him a week later, he handed me a sheet of paper and said, "Here's that one affirmation you wanted!" Sure enough, someone had come up with just one affirmation that covered everything. I have used this for years. It is one of my favorite things to say to myself. The other day I was clearing out some old boxes and I found that piece of paper. It's 32 years old. I had forgotten that it has an explanation of the affirmation. I have no idea who came up with this and the paper doesn't have an author. So, if it was you: thanks!

Here's the affirmation as well as the explanation that was given. The paper calls this "An all-embracing affirmation to speak and to realize."

Everything in my consciousness is in Divine Order.

Everything. Nothing is left out. All aspects, levels and degrees of life as experienced by you are included, just as everything is included in the mind of God. Spiritual understanding, mental clarity, emotional wellness, physical health and function, loving relationships and steady unfoldment in the direction of the fulfillment of destiny are all included.

My Consciousness. Your awareness includes everything because you are in God and God is in you. Your true consciousness is omnipresent as God is omnipresent. Know that God's consciousness and reality is your consciousness and reality.

Divine Order. When we are in harmony within and without, everything literally works together for good – for ideal end results. Therefore, claim Divine Order in your life and affairs. Claim this for your world. Claim this for every person you know and allow them to unfold their innate potential.

It was difficult for an-out-of-work employment consultant to find a job during a recession, but find a job I did! It was with an agency that had been one of my biggest competitors before I had to close my business. They were delighted to have me and I was happy to be with them. They were very nice people.

In my heart, I knew this was a steppingstone job but I didn't know what I was stepping to. I continued my spiritual studies. My inner nun began to reawaken. In fact, I decided I wanted to become a Science of Mind minister and began to aim my studies in that direction.

There's a small area of the United States that many people don't know about. It's called Point Roberts, Washington. When the 49th Parallel was drawn as part of the Oregon Treaty in 1846, this caused a 4.9 square mile area of land to be in the United States, even though it was surrounded by water on three sides and by Canada on the fourth.

Since living in Canada, I had made some friends there. One day, a very dear friend, Ruby Gibson White, who had lived at Point Roberts for years, called me and said there was a job at Point Roberts that she felt I was perfect for: editor of the local newspaper.

"What?" I asked. "I don't know anything about running a newspaper; I'm not qualified for the job."

She said that didn't matter, that what they needed was someone who knew business, could write, and who could relate to people. "You are perfect for the job. Here's the name and number of the person to call." Neither of us knew how guided she was to reach out to me about this job.

I figured I had nothing to lose, shrugged my shoulders, and made the call. I explained who I was and who had referred me for the job.

The publisher was genuinely sorry. "I wish I had known about you yesterday," he said. "We just hired someone and she starts next week."

"Well," I said, "Keep me in mind in case she doesn't work out."

Over the next few months I watched what happened to the newspaper. The woman they had hired was just out of journalism school. Although she was a good writer, it was pretty clear she was immature when it came to people. I started to see angry letters to the editor and the advertising became less each issue. Newspapers survive on advertising so this was not a good thing.

It was almost Christmas. One of the things I had always coached my employment clients to do is stay in touch with people they wanted to work for. You never know when situations will change. So, I took my own advice and bought a gorgeous Christmas card and sent it to the publisher with my best wishes for the new year.

I didn't hear anything back. Little did I know how this Christmas card made me stand out. It was well-known in the area, although not to me, that the owners of the newspaper were Jewish.

I kept up my routine of spiritual reading and meditating first thing in the morning. To this day, it is still the way I begin my day!

The church needed help with their newsletter so I started helping them with it. They needed a church organist so I began to play the organ some Sundays. On the Sundays I didn't go to church, I watched Terry Cole-Whittaker, a New Thought minister from southern California, who had a television show at that time.

My spouse was not happy about this. He didn't understand what I was studying and refused to come with me so he could check it out. He began to say very disparaging things to me such as, "Before I know it, you'll be wearing orange robes and selling flowers in the airport." Of course, he began throwing out the "c" word: cult.

To this day, it amazes me how people will call any spiritual organization a cult if the group is anywhere outside what is accepted by the mainstream. This is so incredibly unfair and it only shows how shallow these people are. Check something out before you label it anything. And realize that, according to some definitions, the biggest cult in the world is organized Christianity!

Of course, there have been and are groups that call themselves religious who are hateful and harmful. Some of these can be called cults. But just because a group has some beliefs that are dissimilar to our own does not automatically make them a cult.

It hurt to be misunderstood. It hurt even more that he didn't care enough to learn more about my interests. I had learned to play golf. Couldn't he at least visit the church once or twice so he could meet the people and see how nice they were?

Naturally, we grew further and further apart. He said maybe we should get a divorce. I said, "Yes, we should." I decided to let him have the house and the furniture, taking only what I had brought into the marriage. He also had to keep the second mortgage debt. He agreed.

While I was packing my things getting ready to move into my new place, I got a phone call from the publisher of the newspaper.

"Our new person isn't working out," he said. "Can you come in for an interview?"

"When," I asked.

"Tomorrow at 6?"

"I will be there."

I went, was interviewed, and was hired.

Two weeks later I had a new job and was living by myself in a small cottage that had been built as a summer home in the 1940s.

I kept studying and meditating and knowing that destiny was calling my name. I just didn't know how.

· · · · ·

Rest Stop

How open are you to ideas that differ from your own? Are you open and flexible about learning new things? Or are you closed and sure you know everything? When we're open to new people and ideas, life is able to give us so much more and our world is enriched.

Can you let other people be who they need to be? Are you willing to let your family members and friends evolve and change, even if it might mean the end of a relationship? It's not uncommon for one person in a relationship to enter a spiritual path while the other person doesn't. This doesn't have to cause problems.

If each person in a relationship respects the other person and their paths in life, two very different people can be in a highly satisfying relationship. It is when one person demands the other to stay the same or to be just like them that troubles begin.

In any relationship, we need to hold on lightly, allow the other person to be who they are, and delight in our differences. There's a reason there are many different kinds of flowers, animals, and plants. God loves diversity!

Not all relationships are meant to last forever. As I think my life – and yours – shows, many of our relationships are not meant to last a lifetime. Sometimes we are with someone for karmic reasons and then we move on. If this happens for you, be willing to be gracious, accept what the relationship has given you, and allow it and yourself to change.

Learning how to run a small newspaper.

The first day on my new job my boss met me at the newspaper office. You see, the owners were over an hour away. To get to the main office I had to drive through a Canadian border into Canada and then through a United States border crossing to re-enter the United States. The border guards on both sides got to know all of us who made this trip on a regular basis. I still lived on the Canadian side so made the trip through the border frequently.

My boss showed me around the tiny one-room office in Point Roberts, showed me where the back issues were, gave me some rate cards for clients, told me when the deadlines were and said to call him if I had questions.

As editor of a small newspaper, I was to do everything: write articles, sell ads, layout the paper, do the distribution, attend government meetings, and be the public relations person for the publication. When he hired me, the publisher said not to worry about learning how to do the graphics production. They would do most of it, but what I needed to know he would teach me.

After he left, I sat there and said to myself, "What have I done? I don't have a clue how to proceed!" Fear gripped me.

I shut my eyes, took a few deep breaths, and asked for guidance.

Then I heard this thought run through my mind, "If I was the editor of a small newspaper, what would I do next?" Ideas came to me and I wrote them down.

- Get out and meet people.
- Ask them what they want in their newspaper.
- Ask them what the most important issues are.
- Find out what meetings I need to attend and why.
- I started doing those things.

When it came time to sell ads, attend county meetings, or write stories, I would do the same thing. I would close my eyes, take a few deep breaths and ask myself, "If I was a writer or a journalist or an ad sales rep, what would I do next?"

Then I would do whatever ideas came to me. This worked beautifully. I always got the information I needed and when I followed the inner guidance I received, things worked out. You would have thought I had done this before.

Because of my various past lives, I am sure I had done all of these jobs before and was drawing on this information to guide me. It wasn't necessarily easy. Parts of this were incredibly challenging. But I was able to call on this guidance and it worked.

I loved this job. I got to do all sorts of things I would never have done otherwise. I got to listen to the police scanner and go to the scene of accidents, interview people, and take pictures. The local volunteer fire department let me come to some of their practice burns and real fires. They made me an honorary firefighter and even gave me a badge I carried in my wallet for years.

And although not everyone liked me, I was able to work well with the various personalities and factions that lived there. I believe my experience interviewing drug addicts and their families as well as job applicants helped me a lot. I knew how to pay attention to people and listen to them in such a way that they knew they had been heard. People felt they could trust and confide in me. Most people were very open and shared some of their secrets. They trusted me when I said something was "off the record" because it was. They felt I didn't judge them even when they knew I didn't agree with their position. And it was true; I didn't judge them.

People who live in Point Roberts get to know the border guards of both countries. One time as I was leaving the Point and driving into Canada, a guard I saw quite a lot came to the car window and asked if I would do him a favor. "Sure," I said.

"Get out of your car and walk around to the back and open your trunk," he said with a smile. "Okay," I said, not knowing what he was up to.

When we got to the back of the car, I opened my trunk. We stood there while he acted like he was going through things in my trunk. All that was there was a bundle of newspapers.

After about two or three minutes of chatting about the weather, he turned to me and said, "This is great. You can go on now. Anyone in the line behind you who is trying to sneak something across the border is scared and it will be easy for me to pick them out of the line."

I smiled, said he was welcome and went on my way. I have always wondered how many unsuspecting folks he got that day.

Eventually, the border guards started asking me which country I was going to live in. I guess they got tired of me going back and forth so much!

I left Canada and moved to Point Roberts. My dear friend Ruby came to the rescue again: she found me the perfect house right across the street from the ocean. The house had a huge floor-to-ceiling window where I could watch the ocean with her various tides, storms, and moon shadows. I spent many hours writing with this delicious view as the backdrop to my thoughts. The view was quite conducive to deep meditations.

I kept feeling an inner urge. This was all taking me somewhere, but I didn't know where. I loved what I was doing and I loved the people at Point Roberts, but something was brewing within and I didn't know what. Then, nine months after I had started the newspaper job, it happened. I got the message I didn't know I was waiting for.

· · · · ·

Rest Stop

Have you tried acting "as if?" This is a powerful manifestation secret also known as living with the assumption that you have or are what you are trying to manifest on the physical plane. Here's why it works:

Everything that exists on the physical plane has to first exist in someone's mind. Think about building a house. First, a person decides what sort of house they want to build. Then they have an architect draw up plans, then the builders follow the plans. Eventually, a house exists where one didn't exist before. All of these people were acting as if the house existed while they were building it.

We don't have the builders just show up and tell them to build a house. What a mess that would be. No, first we draw up the plans. We build the house on paper. Then it becomes a physical reality.

Then next time you're trying to manifest something, get clear on what you want. Then begin acting as if it is already yours, that it already exists. If you do this in earnest, you'll be pleasantly surprised with the results.

My future is revealed.

One day I was driving from Bellingham to Point Roberts when I heard this thought in my head: "Move to Seattle and start a monthly New Age community newspaper."

"What?" I asked.

"Move to Seattle and start a monthly New Age community newspaper." With the statement I was given a visual image of what the newspaper would look like.

At this time, my brother Lou was living in Seattle. We had always been very close and he had been on his metaphysical journey years before I began mine. I called him and told him what had happened. I asked him if he would please drive around Seattle to different metaphysical bookstores and churches, pick up every spiritual or holistic publication he could find, and mail them to me.

He did this and I saw that none of them was like the one I had been shown. I realized this was my next step. This was the calling I had been feeling but couldn't name. I decided I would start a monthly New Age community newspaper.

Ideas started coming to me and I began to write them down. Of course, I realized I would need money to start a business. I didn't have much money. I was recently separated and had walked out with very little. My job at the newspaper didn't pay very much. Where was I to find the money I needed?

I figured I needed about $10,000. I'm still not sure how I came up with that amount, but it's what I thought I would need to move and get started with the first few issues of the newspaper. After that, I thought advertising revenue would start to flow.

I checked in with my bank but they weren't interested in loaning me any money. I looked around at some of my friends who I thought might have money to loan. No one was interested. It got to the point that if I met someone who looked like they had money, I would ask them, "Would you like to invest in a newspaper I'm going to start in Seattle?"

Invariably the answer was, "No."

I began to get frustrated. Since this idea has been dropped into my mind, wasn't someone responsible for providing the material support I required to move to Seattle and start this business?

One day I was feeling particularly discouraged. I opened my mail. There was a newsletter from a local New Thought church. On the front page was the following quote:

> "Until one is committed, there is hesitancy, the chance to draw back. Concerning all acts of initiative (and creation), there is one elementary truth the ignorance of which kills countless ideas and splendid plans: that the moment one definitely commits oneself, then Providence moves too. All sorts of things occur to help one that would never otherwise have occurred. A whole stream of events issues from the decision, raising in one's favor all manner of unforeseen incidents and meetings and material assistance, which no man could have dreamed would have come his way. Whatever you can do, or dream you can do, begin it. Boldness has genius, power, and magic in it. Begin it now."
> (This quote is usually attributed to Johann Wolfgang von Goethe,)

I felt like I had been hit over the head with a brick. I realized that although I was thinking and planning about this business I was going to start, I had not made a definite commitment to the project. I sat for a few minutes, stunned by this realization. Okay, I had to make a commitment.

I picked up the telephone and called my boss.

"Boss," I said, "I am giving you a month's notice that I will be leaving this job and moving to Seattle to start a monthly New Age community newspaper."

"What?" he said. "You can't do that. You don't know what you're doing. You don't know how to publish a newspaper."

"I know," I replied. "But I'm doing it anyway."

When I hung up the phone, I felt a strange mixture of excitement and stark terror. Now not only did I not have the money to start the newspaper, I also didn't have a job. What had I just done?

A part of me expected the skies to open and rain down money on me. After all, I had made a commitment so Providence was supposed to move now, right? That isn't exactly what happened. Nothing is what happened. No sudden calls out of the blue. No new person showed up with a bucket load of cash to give to me.

I quit my job and moved to Seattle to start The New Times in 1985. What a brave soul I was with no idea of the adventure in store for me.

But I was committed and there was a definite shift in my thinking and attitude. I finished up the work with my job while making the necessary plans to move to Seattle. My brother helped me pack the moving truck.

He and a new friend of his were moving into a house together and asked if I wanted to move in with them. Sure, said I. At least I would have a place to land when I got there.

We arrived with my possessions on the Saturday before Easter. The next morning, my brother got angry because his friend made too much noise using an electric can opener to feed her cat. He got so angry that he decided to leave town and move back to Texas. What?

The one support person whom I had counted on was now gone. I was alone in a new city with hardly any money, following my inner guidance to start a spiritual newspaper I called The New Times.

· · · · ·

Rest Stop

This is a great time to address the issues of listening to our inner guidance, taking risks, and making big moves. In some ways what I did was not only risky but foolhardy. Who quits a job and moves to a new city to start a business without capital, contacts, or the right kind of experience?

Trust me, I don't advocate anyone doing this, unless they feel in their heart that they must. Sometimes our inner guidance will stretch us beyond anything we've known before. Sometimes our inner guidance leads us down pathways that are meant to stretch us and make us grow in unseen ways; in ways we can't possibly see ahead of time.

Sometimes our soul-self just has to have its way with us and our job is to cooperate. This is what I did and it was difficult. Would I trade this experience for any other? No. Do I recommend it to you? Maybe.

Learn how to get in touch with your inner guidance. Be sure what you are hearing is true guidance and not the voice of your ego. Then make a commitment to follow your guidance no matter what and see what happens. Start with baby steps in the direction of your dreams and as long as you get positive feedback, keep going in that direction.

I always told myself that the worst that could happen is I would have to get a job again. Instead, a wonderful newspaper was built that helped a lot of people.

Sometimes you have to stretch yourself and take a big step to get to where you're going. If this happens for you, take a deep breath, trust and jump!

The New Times is born.

After my brother left, his friend became my friend and asked if I would like to stay as her housemate. She believed in what I was doing and was walking her own spiritual path. I said I would stay and began my work.

This was in 1985 and it was before the days of computers and cell phones. I made my supporting documents such as rate sheets and writer's guidelines by using a Selectric electric typewriter and press type. What I lacked in sophistication and knowledge, I made up for with spiritual guidance and enthusiasm.

I began going around to the different bookstores and New Thought churches, introducing myself and telling everyone about this newspaper that I was going to publish the next month. Yes, I had given myself a month to get the first issue out.

Although I was received politely by folks, they were not quick to pull out their checkbooks to buy advertising in a newspaper that didn't yet exist. I couldn't blame them; I would feel the same way. "Who is this woman who just breezed into town saying she is starting a spiritual newspaper? What if I buy an ad and the newspaper is never printed?"

But a few brave souls stepped forward and bought ads. The very first ad I got was a $3 classified ad from The Abundant Life Seed Foundation. They didn't become regular advertisers, but I have always carried a fond spot for them in my heart.

To help encourage people, I gave away some ads. I chose a few businesses I thought would be likely to advertise and had ads made up for them and put them in the paper free of charge.

What about articles? Where would those come from? A few people said they would write something and did. But what about the front page story? I didn't know enough people to even have a clue what would make a good front page story.

One Sunday morning as I was meditating, I received the intuitive message to get in my car and drive to a certain New Thought church to attend their service. By now I was getting pretty good at following this inner voice, got in my car and arrived just as the service was starting.

I looked around and wondered why I was there. Shortly after the service started, the minister said there was a guest speaker. My ears perked up. She said a woman named Rama Vernon was involved in taking groups of people to Russia in order to foster peace between our countries. Rama was to speak during the service about what she was doing.

Here is my front page story, I realized. After the service was over, I went up to her, said I was starting a spiritual newspaper and would she be interested in being interviewed for it. She agreed. We set a day, time and place and I got her phone number.

I showed up at the appointed time but she wasn't there. Someone at her house called her and we spoke on the phone. She said she had to get her hair done because she was leaving on a trip to Russia, but if I could come to the hair salon she would still give me an interview.

I hopped into my car and the first interview for The New Times took place in a hair salon with my subject under a hair dryer.

I was having my newspaper printed at my former place of employment and they had told me they would give me 30 days to pay my bill. The day before the paper was to be printed, I got a call saying they wanted half down instead. One of the owners of the printing company didn't like that I had been given 30 days and retracted the offer.

Naturally, I didn't have the money. Fortunately, my new friend and housemate stepped up to the plate and loaned me the money so the first issue could be printed.

I have to admit it was very exciting when that first issue came out. It was small, only eight pages. But by following my inner voice and using my intuitive skills, this newspaper was now a physical reality.

My next hurdle was trying to figure out where I was going to give away 7,000 copies of my newspaper. I knew some obvious locations but I needed many more. I barely knew the city. Another new friend of mine who published a holistic magazine called Insight Northwest, helped me. Over the phone, she gave me a beginning list of places where I could take the newspaper.

Over the next few days, I delivered the free newspaper to many locations and began my distribution lists. One evening soon after, I received a very upsetting phone call.

The phone rang and I answered it. An angry woman on the other end of the line proceeded to tell me how awful I was. She said I was the Anti-Christ and that I was destined to face the fires of hell. I listened, tried to reason with her, and realized there was nothing I could say she would listen to. Eventually, I told her I was hanging up the phone and did so.

About an hour later, the phone rang again. A New Thought minister who had written an article in the first issue said, "I just got a phone call."

"The Anti-Christ?" I asked.

"You, too?" he said with a laugh in his voice.

"Yes, me, too," I responded.

We spent some time on the phone and he gave me a great perspective. He said people like this woman don't bother with you unless they think you will make a difference. He congratulated me and said to be happy someone felt so threatened right away.

This reminded me of the first time I had received a negative letter to the editor at the newspaper in Point Roberts. My boss said that I should never be upset about negative comments. Why? Because everyone will never agree with you on everything so whether you receive negative or positive comments, it is good. It means people are reading the newspaper.

This attitude has helped me numerous times and I have shared it with other writers and business people.

If you are doing anything of value that can be seen by other people, you will be criticized. Some people will think they could do your job better than you can (and maybe they could). Others will think they know more than you do (and maybe they do). They will feel compelled to share this with you.

If you are being criticized, rejoice! Someone is noticing you and your work. It doesn't matter whether or not they like you or your work. There will never come a time when everyone will agree with you, understand you, or like you. None of that matters if you are living in alignment with your soul calling.

A few years ago, I received an email from a man who told me he would never advertise in my current newspaper, New Spirit Journal, because I teach meditation classes. He said it is unfair because I can advertise my classes free and the advertisers can't do that. He also said he had discussed this with a group of 30 other people and they all agreed with him that they would never advertise with me for this reason.

My heart felt sad and my stomach churned to think he and 30 other people had been discussing me and felt this way.

I emailed him back and said I was confused by his email because I don't and never have taught meditation classes. I also said I was sorry he had any sort of negative feelings toward me or my business.

He responded with more negativity without addressing the fact that he was mistaken about his core complaint: my teaching meditation classes. At that point I realized there was some other issue bothering him and I was best advised to wish him well and move on. So I did and I still don't know what his true issue with me was or is.

A few weeks after the first issue of The New Times came out, I received a copy of that issue sent anonymously in the mail. The newspaper was marked up in red ink throughout. Any typo I had missed was circled and there were many suggestions of how this person would have edited the articles.

My first reaction was to feel terrible. I was doing my best and I felt I had done a good job. Here was someone I didn't even know who hid behind the shield of anonymity criticizing this first issue of my newspaper. He or she didn't even give me the opportunity to defend myself or my decisions.

This time I felt a little stronger, took the paper, and burned it to rid myself of that energy. As I did this, I reminded myself to rejoice because The New Times was being noticed and read, which is why I was publishing it in the first place!

· · · · ·

Rest Stop

How do you handle criticism? It's impossible to navigate our way though life without criticism from ourselves or others. If you find yourself being judgmental and critical of yourself, say, "Cancel, cancel, love, love." You are doing the best you can. If you can do better, do so. Wallowing in self-criticism doesn't help anyone.

If other people criticize you, tell them they might be right. Don't argue with them. Consider what the person said. If it has value, make some adjustments. If it doesn't have value, let it go and move on.

Some people thrive on being critical. If you are doing something creative, some of these folks will be drawn to you. By being critical of your work they feel they are absolved from doing their own. Some people will be jealous of you especially if you are successful. Bless them and let them go.

As I learned, if you're being criticized it means your work is being noticed. Rejoice!

The early days.

After the first issue was published, it was a little easier to approach people because I had something to show them. Most loved the paper right away and many wanted to be a part of it. Some wanted to write articles, some felt they should be interviewed by me, and a few wanted to advertise.

It was, however, a very challenging time. It seems nothing came easily, especially in the area of finances. I felt I was walking through Jello. I had no support other than the income from the newspaper and I lived day to day, not even month to month. There were times when I had less than $5 to my name.

What was humorous to me is that when I divorced my husband, I kept his car, a white Toronado. This was not an inexpensive car. My ex-husband had a company vehicle from his employer at the time and he had sold my 1975 Ford Mustang without my permission, so this is how I ended up with a car I would never have purchased on my own.

The hilarious part is that people thought I had money when they saw the car I drove. They didn't know I could barely keep gas in it. Before long, I traded it in for a used pick-up truck so I would be able to deliver the newspaper more easily.

Once when I went to interview someone, he saw my little truck, scrunched up his nose at me and asked, "Why is a nice young woman like you driving a pick-up truck like this?"

"Because I need to be able to deliver my newspapers," I responded smiling. I thought it very interesting that he looked on my truck with such disdain.

This taught me early on that even though my work was in a spiritually-oriented field, people were still full of judgments and made such judgments based on external appearances. I learned not to correct people when they thought I had a lot of money because I wanted to succeed and make money.

I realized that every time I corrected someone to say, "Oh, no, I don't have a lot of money; I got this car in a divorce," I was affirming lack of money. Instead, I would not make any comment at all when people alluded to my financial status. Truly it wasn't their business anyway!

The second issue of The New Times brought another sharp lesson. I had worked hard and picked up some new advertisers and many new readers. It was encouraging that people resonated with what I was doing immediately. I wanted to do a good job and provide the best publication I was capable of producing.

Imagine my dismay when I received the second issue and it had a huge typo... in the headline! The article was about a local New Age Church. Instead of the word "church," the headline read "chruch." This was in huge print. In the headline. In my second issue of the paper.

I was humiliated and embarrassed. I had 7,000 copies of this newspaper and there was no way to do a reprinting. Not only wasn't there time to do another printing, I couldn't have afforded it. The error was mine. Even though two people had proofed the paper, this error made its way through the printing process.

I wanted to dump all 7,000 copies in the river and pretend it had not been printed. But I knew I couldn't do that; people were expecting this issue to be distributed the next day.

When I got back to my office and started looking at the paper, I realized that the reason the typo had occurred was because our eyes tend to fill in what we think we see. I decided to try an experiment. I took a copy of the paper and showed it to five people, independently of one another. I said, "Can you tell me if there is a typo on this page?"

Remember, it was in the headline - this sentence was the biggest one on the page. I watched their eyes scan the page. Not one of them found the typo, even with me telling them one was there! I relaxed because I realized that most people wouldn't see it. And I realized that the paper would be replaced in a month with a new issue.

So although it was humiliating and it made me try even harder to have no errors, I also realized that I didn't have to focus on my mistakes and that if I didn't focus on them, others wouldn't pay as much attention either. This was a perfect lesson in "energy flows where our attention goes." I focused on people reading the articles and finding strength and inspiration rather than on them seeing the typo and making fun of me.

Although no one ever mentioned it, I was very happy when I could put out another issue and have that one recede to the archives.

Although this certainly made me even more diligent about typos, I have learned they sometimes occur, even though we have three proofings of each issue. When we do make a mistake, I always regret it but I also have learned to let it go as soon as I can.

Disillusionment sets in

When I began The New Times, I was a "newby" at New Age thinking. In fact, I was surprised that I was the one guided to publish such a newspaper. Quickly, I began to meet people who knew a lot more than I did. I hid my feelings of being an outsider since I didn't know very much about New Age thinking. I considered myself more part of the New Thought movement that I perceived as having a more spiritual base. I still planned to become a New Thought minister.

It didn't take long for that to change. Three things happened to wake me up pretty quickly. Just because people said they were on a spiritual path didn't mean it was so.

One of the first things that happened was when I went to an appointment to see a New Thought minister. I wanted to tell him what I was doing and see if he would like to write some articles or advertise. The day I went to see him was a warm one and I was wearing a cool but very modest dress.

When I walked into his office, he stood up, came around the desk, took my hand and while looking me up and down said, "Well, look at you, wearing such a nice feminine dress." What did that have to do with anything? Later I learned he had quite an eye for the ladies and never tried to hide it, even from his wife. It sure felt creepy and inappropriate to me. I have not worn a dress to business meetings since that day.

The second thing happened when I went to drop off a new issue of the newspaper at another New Thought church. The paper was free and it said "free" right at the top of the front page. I found my newspapers in a basket with a sign saying, "50 cents." Here I was barely able to pay my rent and buy food, and this church was using my free publication to make money for themselves.

I took the papers and the sign and didn't leave any new issues. When I asked about it in the bookstore, I received shrugging shoulders with some sort of comment about them being a non-profit. To which I replied, "So am I but without the benefits you enjoy!"

My third big disillusionment with a New Thought church came when I attended a prosperity class. There were about 15 students who showed up for the class. The teacher began by asking us to each say what we were trying to manifest.

Different people said things such as cars, jobs, and spouses. I was honest when she came to me and I said, "I want to manifest consciously being in the presence of God all the time. If I can manifest that, everything else will fall into place. 'Seek ye first the Kingdom and all these other things will be added'."

The teacher looked at me in silence for a few heartbeats and then she said dismissively, "Well, the rest of us aren't as advanced as you are so we're going to work on manifesting cars and jobs."

How sorry I was for what I said. I wished I could disappear. I felt ashamed and realized that how I viewed spirituality and manifesting was quite different from how these folks viewed it. I didn't say anything else in the class and didn't go back. Many times I have wished I knew the name of the teacher. I would love to talk to her and get her perspective.

I realized that some people saw, and still do see, New Age or New Thought spirituality as a way to get as much materiality as they can. It's as if the techniques of affirmation, visualization, and others are meant only to make our lives on the earth plane better. It's as if spirituality has nothing to do with God other than God being some kind of huge vending machine. We put in an affirmation or two and out pops a car. Put in a few visualizations and out pops a new spouse or job!

I am so happy that the first New Thought minister I studied with taught from a spiritual viewpoint. This was one of the reasons I felt so at-home in my first spiritual group. Had I started out in one of these others, I might not have stayed around.

Although I have come across some wonderful New Thought groups since these early days and even belong to one, I think there are still many of them that try too hard to bend to people's lower natures rather than trying to lead people to higher planes. Many of the teachings have melted into the mainstream. On the surface this seems to be a good thing.

What happens in many cases is that once these ideas hit the mainstream, they are watered down so people will accept them rather than helping people rise to new levels. I do understand the thinking behind this and I think it is a mistake.

The church I attend, Ananda Church of Self-realization, doesn't do this and I appreciate it so much. One Sunday not too long ago, I was talking to a gentleman who had been going to a different church. He said, "What I like so much about Ananda is the sense of devotion I feel here. With the other church I attended, they were trying so hard to reach the young people that the services were more like rock music concerts. I just couldn't take it any more."

Every church and group has to do what they feel led to do and I am sure that some of them are doing a fine job of attracting young people or hooking people who think they just want to improve their material lives. There's nothing wrong with that. Spirituality does help us improve our physical lives. It also does much, much more than that!

The "Seek ye first" statement doesn't say "Seek ye only…and that is all you'll get." It says, "…and all these other things will be added." It truly is the full package when we approach it in that way!

"We expect to read – and hear – great things from you."

One of the things I didn't know when I started The New Times was that I would be expected to write an inspirational column every month. When that tidbit of information trickled into my mind, I was quite surprised. What could I write about? How could I put myself into the role of a teacher even on a small level when I was still such a student?

During the first year when finances were so terrible, a colleague invited me to a channeling session where she said the Ascended Masters would speak to the group. If you aren't familiar with channeling, this is when a disembodied person speaks through someone who does have a body.

There are different kinds of channels and not all of them actually take control of the person's body. Many don't do that. Instead, they give mental dictation and the channel hears the words internally and then speaks them aloud. In fact when I had first began to meditate, I had this experience with a being who called himself Silver Owl.

I would sit down with pen in hand and ask questions about various issues and then write down what I heard. Some pretty interesting information came through. These days a lot of people channel and it is important to try to be sure the source of the information isn't just a disembodied entity trying to have some fun.

As I tell people, if your Uncle Harry always got into trouble and pulled pranks when he was alive, chances are he's doing the same thing from the other side! Use your discernment.

Sometimes the information is coming from a person's own subconscious mind. Not all the information a person receives is valid. Some of it is just garbage. Use your discernment.

The Ascended Masters are a group of beings who have mastered themselves and this world, who have reached God-realization, and who are committed to helping the rest of us find our way to such mastery. They are called masters because they have mastered themselves and have realized their true essence. Some people have difficulty using the word "master" because they think this means we are saying the person is master over us.

Not so. It is similar to calling a master musician Maestro or saying someone is a master builder, master chef, or master of some sort of sport. Using the term master is being respectful and honoring the person's accomplishments.

At this event, we were allowed to ask questions. I asked, "Will my newspaper The New Times succeed? It is so difficult for me that sometimes I don't think this is what I should be doing."

The woman who was channeling had her eyes closed and she began to smile, chuckled, nodded her head in the affirmative, and said, "Oh, yes. It will succeed beyond your wildest dreams. And we expect to read – and hear – a lot of wisdom from you. You will write and teach through this vehicle you have formed. Don't worry. All will be well."

I felt consoled, of course. But I did wonder about the writing part. Again, what did I have to say? As for the speaking part, I detested getting up in front of people to speak. This was so bad for me that I would get nauseous and turn red when I had to get up in front of others to speak.

Fortunately for me, I had joined Toastmasters for a year and had learned a lot about public speaking from that organization. I still recommend to clients that they get involved in Toastmasters. It not only teaches you about public speaking, but about leadership and how to relate to people in an effective way.

Each month as it came time to write my editorial, I would sit quietly, close my eyes and ask for a topic. Eventually, one would come to me. I put my fingers on the keyboard and started writing. Information flowed to me. I wasn't channeling, but I was tapping into another part of myself that had things to say.

I have to admit that sometimes I did feel I was receiving information from spiritual guides and teachers from another dimension. Sometimes I was quite surprised at what I had written and wondered where the thoughts had come from.

Eventually, to my surprise, my articles became one of the most popular columns in the newspaper. My initial dedication to providing information that would help people lead happier lives came to mean information from myself as well as others.

After awhile I published a collection of these in a book called *Comments on Leading the Spiritual Life*. It is out of print now but occasionally can be found in used bookstores or online.

The community steps up to help me

Besides writing articles and interviews, I also took photos to go with the stories. One day I came home to discover someone had broken into the house and stolen my camera. Nothing else in the home was taken, not even anything that belonged to the other person who lived there.

Not only did I feel violated, I felt targeted. Who disliked me – or was threatened by me – so much that they would steal one of the tools I needed to produce the newspaper?

When some of my new friends heard what happened, they got together and took up a collection. They raised enough money for me to replace my camera! That felt amazing to me and I was incredibly grateful to them. I even wrote an article about it, saying that this is the spirit of our spiritual community to reach out and help one another.

I never did find out who stole the camera, but I did forgive them and moved on.

Wayne Dyer contacts me

This was 1985, before Dr. Wayne Dyer was as famous as he is today and well before he had written as many books as he has. In fact, I barely knew who he was when I got a letter from him. He wanted to know if I would send him the names and addresses of people who subscribed to my newspaper so he could send them a free copy of his book *Gifts From Eykis.*

This was before he was famous, so forgive my initial response to him. I asked if he was doing this just to build his mailing list. Why should I share these names and addresses with him? He would get in touch with them trying to sell them something and that didn't feel good to me.

This was before email and the internet, by the way. We were conversing through snail mail. Wayne wrote back, saying that, yes, he was building his mailing list but by offering them a free book at no charge to myself, I could also build mine.

He felt real and genuine to me so I agreed. When I started the paper, I had no idea people would subscribe. I had intended it to be totally free so people wouldn't have to decide whether or not they wanted to pay for the uplifting information that was in it. But I did offer the choice of having the paper mailed for a small fee, enough to cover the postage.

Once The New Times got rolling, I was able to meet and interview some of the early pioneers of the New Age community. People like Deepak Chopra, Wayne Dyer, Marianne Williamson and others came to my office for interviews. It was a time of expansion for all of us.

As subscriptions came in, I wrote down the names and addresses on a sheet of paper and mailed it to Wayne. On the subscription form in the paper, I gave people the choice of receiving his book or not. Most wanted the book and I'm sure this offer helped both of us build our lists of people who were interested in what we were doing.

When Wayne came to town later that year, I was invited to the home of his host. In those days, Wayne and I both still drank beer and I still smoked cigarettes. I remember standing around in the kitchen with him and a number of others, talking, laughing and drinking our beers.

At one point, I went outside to have a cigarette. I was sitting on a large rock when Wayne came outside. Since I had been judged by the spiritual community about being a smoker, I was ready for more. He said to me, "I love seeing smokers smoking."

"Really? Why? So you can convert them to being non-smokers?" Ouch!

"No," he laughed. "Because I like seeing people enjoy themselves!"

"Oh," was all I could say in return.

I don't know how long we kept the free book offer going, but it was for several years. When Wayne's book, *I Can See Clearly Now*, came out in 2014, it was a lot of fun for me to read about how he decided to write and publish Gift From Eykis and to appreciate the small part The New Times played in helping him make the book better known.

During these early years of The New Times, people such as Wayne Dyer, Deepak Chopra, Louise Hay, and others would travel around giving large group seminars. They usually advertised these events in my newspaper.

One time when Wayne and Deepak Chopra were giving a local seminar, they were being represented by a man whose name I don't remember. This man took out advertising that added up to $1,000. Usually I didn't (and still don't) take ads without payment. The issue with advertising is if you don't get your payment up front, you have no leverage to getting paid. The ad is out and distributed doing its job. It can't be repossessed. Besides, as I like to tell people, I am not running a bank that gives loans. Look at me like the grocery store. You walk in, get your groceries, pay and leave.

In this case, the fellow talked me into giving him credit because of who he was representing. He didn't pay when he said he would. When the event came to town, I went to it and saw the tables of products Wayne and Deepak were selling. On top of the income from the seminar that cost several hundred dollars per person, they were raking in the dough selling their products.

I still had not been paid for the ad and it was beginning to really feel unfair to me. I sat down and wrote Wayne a letter, telling him what happened. I asked him, "Do you have any idea what it felt like for me to see all those people there at your event knowing they had paid a lot of money to be there and buying your products, and here I was a little nobody not getting paid. It just feels so unfair!"

I asked him if he would please talk to the fellow who represented him and ask him to pay his bill.

A few weeks later I got a letter from Wayne and in it was a check for $1,000, asking me to please tell the fellow that Wayne had handled his bill for him.

I was blown away. I had no idea he would do this and to this day I appreciate his integrity in stepping up even though he had not made the contract with me.

Help from an unknown benefactor

Have I said how difficult this time was for me, especially financially? I thought I had mentioned it. One time, twice actually, I received help in a most unusual way.

Before moving to Seattle and starting the newspaper, one of the books I had read was *Strangers Among Us* by Ruth Montgomery. This book is about the concept of walk-ins: souls who are not the original inhabitants of a body. The theory says that when someone has a violent or sudden death, sometimes one soul leaves and another enters. Usually, it is said, the soul entering has some particular work to do here to better the planet.

One such walk-in mentioned in the book was Ruth Soderstrum who owned and operated the Psychic Energy Center in Tacoma, Washington. Not long after I started the newspaper, Ruth got in touch with me and invited me to her center. I met her and saw what she was doing.

What a delightful soul she was! She wanted to know how I was doing financially, so I told her how miserable things were for me. Of course, she already knew that, but had wanted to meet me so she could check me out.

Ruth said she had been contacted by an older gentleman. He offered her some financial assistance. He had read about her in the book and felt drawn to help her. He said he was well-off financially and felt inspired to support people who were trying to do good work in the world. He also wanted to know if she knew of anyone else who needed financial assistance. She decided I was one of those people. I suspect there were others she told him about but I didn't ask.

Ruth told me to write a letter to this man. She told me his name was Bernard. No last name was given. She was going to visit him somewhere in another state and was going to take my letter with her. She said I should tell him about my project, why I was doing it, what my financial situation was, and ask for his help.

This was an exciting prospect for me and receiving some financial assistance would mean a lot. I had no idea how much money Bernard was thinking of giving but any amount would be helpful.

A little bit of time passed and one day I received an envelope in the mail from Ruth. In it was a brief letter and a check written on her account in the amount of $2,500. She said Bernard was giving me this to support my work.

I was overwhelmed with gratitude that someone who didn't even know me would give me $2,500. This was around the same time that my camera had been stolen and it became imperative for me to move. I was able to use some of the funds to move and the rest of it to pay the printing bill that had grown larger than it should have. There is another story about that I will tell you in a minute.

A few months after this, Ruth sent me another check for $2,500 from Bernard. He told her he believed these two checks would be all the help I needed from him because he felt the newspaper would be self-supporting pretty soon.

I don't know if I can properly share with you how amazing this experience was for me, and how much it taught me about the power of following your heart and your dreams even when it seems you cannot succeed. From a purely physical point of view, The New Times should never have existed.

I didn't have proper financial backing, the right kind of experience, any business contacts. I should have failed. Yet, because I followed my inner guidance, was laser-focused in my intentions, was willing to take risks, willing to be the fool and fail, support came in a most wonderful and unexpected way.

About that printing bill...

I couldn't pay the printer

One of the most expensive parts of operating a newspaper is paying the printer. When I started The New Times I was able to get credit from the printer who had owned the small newspaper I operated in Point Roberts. Because I had worked for them they knew and trusted me. However, as I mentioned earlier, at first they had told me they would give me credit for the entire amount for 30 days. The day before I was to print the first issue, they wanted half down. I didn't have the money, but was able to borrow it from a new friend. Then month-to-month, I would pay as much as I could. After a few months, though, my printing bill had grown. I was only able to pay about half or less every month. Finally, I was told that unless I brought $1,000 with me the next time the paper was to be printed, they would not print it. I had 30 days to come up with $1,000 in addition to the money I needed to operate the company, for rent, food, and other living expenses that were minimal but still existed.

I had no idea how I could do this. I asked people I barely knew if they would lend me the money but everyone said no. The night before I was to go to the printer I was so sad. I didn't have the money. I had worked all month long "as if" I would have the money because I honestly thought I would have it.

I cried that night because I had worked very hard to make the paper the success it was becoming and people were starting to depend on the newspaper and the information it provided. I honestly couldn't believe that I would have been allowed to go as far as I had only to have to close the business down now. I went to bed wondering where my miracle would come from and doubting it would come at all.

I got up at 3 a.m. the next morning to drive the sixty miles to the printers. When I showed up I said hello to the people in the typesetting department. I noticed that the person who had given me the ultimatum wasn't there yet. I asked where he was. "Oh, he's out today, playing golf," I was told. "Is he coming in at all?" I asked. "No, he isn't."
I was stunned and stood there for a few heartbeats. No one was asking for the $1,000 dollars. "Okay," I said, "I guess we'll get a move on and get this baby printed." And off I headed to the pressroom where the paper was printed. Within a few hours, the back of my car was full of 10,000 copies of the newspaper. I had gotten my miracle after all! I didn't need money to get that issue printed. By acting "as if" all month long, and by believing I would be provided for, I was. This is, of course, a huge manifestation technique I learned first hand!

This only took care of the one month's printing. The next day I received a call from the fellow at the printer who wanted to know where the $1,000 was. I told him I didn't have it and, besides, he hadn't been there. I heard a big sigh from him and then, "You had better get your account paid in full by next month or we have to stop printing your paper."
I had no idea what I would do. I decided to just keep on doing my work, pray for guidance, and continue to trust. A few days later, I had a phone call from a salesman at a different printing company. He wanted to know what it would take to get me to switch printers. (Not much, I thought to myself.)

"You would have to at least match what I'm paying now and also extend 30-days credit for each issue," I told him. He said he thought he could do that and asked if he could take me to lunch. Things just kept getting better. Now I was getting a free meal, too!

We met for lunch, went over the details, and I had a new printer for the next issue without having to have any cash in hand. Whew.

Of course, I still had to pay the former printing bill and I did need the money to do that. This is about the time Bernard gave me $2,500 which I used to pay the printing bill. What's important to realize is I did not have to have the money when I thought I did in order to keep my business alive. The Universe/God has amazing ways to handle things and I learned that frequently the way things work out is not at all the way we think they will happen. If we are following our path, doing our inner work, praying and meditating to receive guidance and then following it, the Universe will take care of us.

This can be difficult to do; no one said it would be easy. I have learned that the more often we do this, though, the easier it gets. Learning to trust is a process.

• • • • •

Rest Stop

Is there something in your life you are not doing because you think you don't have the experience or the money or the whatever to do it?

Please don't let this stop you. We live in a world of our own making. Over and over I have learned that when I make a move, the universe morphs itself to match my move.

When I sit on my hands – while wringing them, of course – nothing happens. If you don't make your move, the Universe doesn't know you're serious and does nothing.

Whatever it is you want to do, focus your energies, make a plan, and do it. Then adjust as you move forward and see what glorious things are in store for you!

People step up to help me.

There is no way I could have succeeded without the help of numerous volunteers who stepped forward to help me.

One day after I had been in business about eight months, the phone rang. A woman said she wanted to volunteer to help me. Because I had had some rather flaky callers right from the beginning, I was cautious and asked her why she would want to volunteer.

The caller said she had a good job and made enough money, was on her spiritual path and felt it was important to volunteer. She had been reading The New Times, enjoyed it, and felt she would like to help.
My intuition gave me a resounding "Yes," so I told her to come in so we could meet. Thus began a 10-year relationship with one of the best volunteers I have ever known. Mary would come in three times a week and handle my growing subscriber list. She also came in on distribution day and helped with that.

We got to know one another over the years and shared our spiritual and psychological processes of growth and exploration. To this day, I value everything she did for the business and for me as a friend and I know this was a reciprocal relationship.

There were others who contacted me and wanted to help. Although I have always been a volunteer in some capacity, I honestly had not thought about people helping me in this way. I was honored that people saw the value of what I was doing and wanted to be a part of it.

We used to have a wonderful time at distribution. The truck would show up from the printer and thousands of newspapers would be brought into the office. Together we would stick labels on the ones that went out in the mail, bundle up the ones that got sent out to stores, and make stacks of papers for the distributors who would pick them up and take them out to the various locations where the papers were given away free.

I had gone from doing everything myself to having a team of volunteers who came in and helped me. I always provided coffee and donuts and I'm sure the caffeine and sugar helped us move a lot faster and raised our spirits!

On delivery day, a team of volunteers came to my office where we sorted newspapers and got them ready for delivery to over 600 locations. The coffee, donuts, and laughter flowed freely.

One of the dear souls who stepped up to help me was transgendered. I'll call her Louise. Until I met her, I had not had a transgendered friend. In case this is a word you are not familiar with, a transgendered person is someone who identifies with and expresses a different gender than the one they were born with. It has nothing to do with one's sexual orientation. Some transgendered people eventually have surgery to change their physical body to match the gender they feel within. Many don't have the surgery but do dress, live, and act opposite to their physical gender.

When she was a young man, Louise had been quite macho and even played professional baseball. For years she had known something wasn't "right" and eventually figured out what was going on.

Louise had the surgery to transform physically into a woman. But she was very tall and big-boned. She had quit taking some of the medications that would help make her voice higher so had to artificially raise her voice to sound more feminine.

Because we became friends, I had the honor of learning more about the transgendered community and the long, hard road most of these great souls walk.

Louise and I frequently went out for meals together and I got to experience what she went through second hand by watching how people treated her. She didn't pass for a woman very well so people tended to stare at her. One time we had gone out for dinner at a diner and there were some policemen there. They watched us like they expected us to do something wrong any second.

We had a cup of coffee and decided to leave. It wasn't worth running the risk that these officers might decide to turn our evening upside down. I realized that although I only experienced these sorts of things when I was with her, she had to go through them all the time.

Eventually, Louise fell in love and moved across the country. She wrote to me sometimes but we eventually lost touch. I regret that.

A few years later I received a phone call from her partner saying they had split up and she had just received a call saying Louise had killed herself. She used a gun, shot her dog and then herself.

She was not able to make the new life for herself that she had hoped for and this made me very sad. She deserved to live a happy life and wasn't able to do it.

I have often thought that we can learn a lot from the transgendered community. Those of us who believe in reincarnation know that we come back in various lifetimes as male and female. Imagine living both within the same lifetime, at the same time in history and culture. What a soul-learning experience this can be.

Yet, it has been my experience that many transgendered people are tortured souls who are not always healed by the transition they make. Theirs is certainly a unique journey, one their friends and family need to support and help however they can.

We all come here for different reasons and none of us can truly know what a soul's goals are when they come in. All we can do is support one another.

I think Louise was a very spiritual soul who got lost along the way because suicide is generally not the best way to leave. I also know she is fine and will find her way once again. Who knows, maybe we will meet again.

Rest Stop

Volunteering is one of the best ways to grow one's soul as well as to learn about new areas of life, meet and make new friends, and make a genuine contribution to society.

People who are out of work are well-advised to find somewhere to volunteer. More than one person has found a job this way. You never know who else volunteers where you do; people have been known to meet their new boss this way.

People have also ended up being hired where they volunteer because a job came open, the person applied, and there was a verifiable work history the employer knew they could count on.

In today's economic climate, for-profit companies and non-profits alike can benefit from willing volunteers.

I sell my baby.

The next 11 years operating The New Times were some of the best and happiest years of my life. I was living my dream. I was making a difference in the lives of thousands of people. I was fulfilling my soul's calling.

I met and interviewed some of the best-known teachers and authors. In those days when someone came out with a new book, their publishing house sent them on tours. The authors went to many different cities where they were on television and radio programs, interviewed by the print media, and gave classes and lectures.

The New Times was on the list for the Seattle area. People like Deepak Chopra, Marianne Williamson, Wayne Dyer, Iyanla Vanzant, Larry Dossey, Ram Dass, Shakti Gawain, Julia Cameron, and many others came to my office and I interviewed them. It was a wonderful time and I was very grateful to have built the business to this level.

Our readership was over 40,000 people and covered the United States as well as Canada. This was before the internet so people had to read the print edition and couldn't read it online.

Even though my business was doing well and I had grown into being a pretty good writer as well as giving some classes and workshops, I began to get what I called itchy feet. I felt I was supposed to be doing something more with my life. I felt like I should be spending more time writing and teaching.

My partner Rhonda also worked in the business and she was working six to seven days a week. We commuted three or four hours a day because of where we lived. How could we change things so she could have more time off, we wouldn't have to commute so much, and I would be able to spend more time writing?

I thought that maybe it was time to sell the business and start a new one closer to home. At that time the hobby of rubber stamping was huge. It was a hobby we both enjoyed and we were good at it. We decided to sell The New Times and open a rubber stamp hobby shop closer to home. The plan was to get the store up and running and then Rhonda would run the store while I spent my time backing her up and writing and teaching.

It took awhile but we found a buyer for the business. What's interesting is that during this time, all sorts of things happened to slow down the process. I kept getting "no's" in many different ways, but didn't heed them. Once the business had been sold and I had a few weeks off, I regretted my decision and realized I had been getting messages to slow the process down but had ignored them.

We opened our store, StampMagic, in Monroe, Washington. At first, it was great and we enjoyed our new venture. It didn't take long, though, for the realities of retailing to hit us. Not only didn't we have more time off, we actually had to work even more hours than before.

I had forgotten what it was like to start a new business. Not only that but to start a new business in which I had no experience. What was I thinking?

The store lasted about a year. We had invested everything from the sale of The New Times into StampMagic and we had used our credit cards to stay in business as long as we did. Naturally, I beat myself up for this.

I should have known better. My prior business experience should have kept me from letting this happen. Why didn't I invest the money from the sale of The New Times? Why did I take it all and roll the dice on a retail store in a small town?

Why, why, why?

Once we closed the store, Rhonda went to work in the graphics field at the local newspaper. Finding a job was much more difficult for me.

Many companies don't want to hire someone who has owned their own business because it is pretty well known that once you've been in business for yourself you won't be happy until you are an entrepreneur again.

One day I saw a classified ad for marketing director at a retirement community. The moment I saw the ad, I knew this was my next job. Although I didn't have experience in elder care, I have always loved seniors and have always gotten along well with them. I interviewed for the job and a few days later, it was mine.

This began eight years working in the elder care field.

Caring for our elders.

This was 1998 and the field of eldercare was just starting to open up. Nursing homes had been around for a long time, but the social model of retirement and assisted living communities was in its infancy. I was at home in the industry immediately.

The seniors could feel that I genuinely enjoyed them and that I was interested in their being happy. Even some of the most challenging residents eventually came around to respecting me and the position I held.

Eventually, I worked my way to becoming general manager of a community that, under my leadership, grew from 80 apartments to 125, plus including five stand-alone houses and a dementia care building. I oversaw the kitchen, the housekeeping, activities, assisted care, and the growth of the community. It was like being responsible for a small village.

I had a staff of 50 people who reported to department heads who, in turn, reported to me. I had to learn about the various issues faced by people who are aging as well as the rules and regulations of the state government.

State inspectors would come in for site visits and examine every facet of the facility. It was very intimidating. However, the people I worked with at the state level knew I cared and knew I wanted to do a good job. My last year at the community we received the first "no complaint" state ruling ever received by that company.

I was pleased with my staff for making this happen and I was pleased with myself that I had grown so much in this field that I was able to be the leader who supported it happening.

During this time, I also became involved in the wider eldercare community and was on the board of directors for the local senior center as well as holding a position on the county's Council on Aging. One of the areas that became a challenge for me was reporting to the head office of the company I worked for.

When I began work with them, they had 13 communities. Now four years later, they had almost 50. Money became more and more important to the owners. Although I understood they had investors they had to report to, it became increasingly difficult for me to have my work overwhelmingly tied to money and to the other communities rather than to the care of our residents.

For instance, one year my community made a nice profit. Instead of being able to put that money back into my own community, it was sent to one that was having trouble. My staff and I – and thus the residents – had to tighten our belts, even though we had done a great job of managing the finances. And the real turning of the knife in the heart came when the general manager of the community receiving our financial help was recognized for having the best community in the company that year. She could never have done that without the financial support that came from our community. My staff and I were not acknowledged in any way.

Around this same time, the executive director's position at the local senior center came open. This was a non-profit corporation. Because I was on the board of directors, I had a good sense of how things were run. I decided to apply for the position and move into the world of non-profit elder care.

The next four years were spent managing and growing the senior center. It was an incredibly challenging job and forced me to grow in even more ways than the retirement community did.

Over these eight years of working in eldercare, I stayed in touch with the spiritual community in a very loose fashion. Eventually I started receiving phone calls and letters asking me to start another newspaper.

New Spirit Journal is born.

People said they missed the spiritual component that I had brought to the newspaper publishing world. Although I had thought I would never return to the world of publishing, I began to wonder if these calls and emails were a sign from Spirit that I was to return to the world of spiritual publishing.

Because I enjoyed my work with the senior center, it was difficult to even consider returning to publishing. I had to admit, though, that printer's ink does get into one's system and I had been missing the world of the printing press.

Rhonda, my life partner (who in 2013 became my wife after 25 years together), and I thought about it and talked about it. Eventually we decided to start another newspaper. I had fulfilled my five-year no-compete clause that had been part of the sale of The New Times. It had been eight years so I was in total integrity and, in fact, the folks I had sold the paper to had since sold it to someone else and it was now in its third incarnation and serving a different niche than the one we felt called to serve.

In May, 2005, New Spirit Journal was born. This was 20 years since I had started The New Times, to the month! I couldn't help making comparisons between how the two publications were starting. So different yet so much the same.

This time I didn't quit my job. We began New Spirit Journal part-time and both of us kept our day-jobs. This is, as many entrepreneurs know, a difficult way to grow a business. Not only is it physically draining, not being able to put 100% of the energy into the business makes it slower going.

Although the business didn't grow as quickly as we would have liked, it did grow and people let us know how happy they were that we had returned to the scene. After about a year, we decided I needed to move to the business fulltime or it would not be able to make the next leap of growth.

I took a deep breath, planned as best I could and jumped.

It was great being back in publishing and it was scary. A lot had changed between 1996 and 2005. Whereas such things as yoga and feng shui were considered odd and offbeat in 1996, now these words and concepts had found their way into the mainstream. This was and is a mixed blessing.

What seems to happen when spiritual concepts go mainstream is they are watered down and monetized. Instead of being the basis for one's spiritual practice, yoga has become an exercise and/or a way to meet possible dating partners. There are even studios that specialize in naked yoga.

On one television show which explored meditation and mainstream yoga, the question was posed to several teachers: "Why don't you teach the spiritual aspects of yoga?"

One teacher said, "Oh, if they stick with it long enough they will figure that out for themselves."

Some people in the metaphysical community didn't and don't want to have anything to do with a publication that has the word spirit in the title. I have been told by some yoga studios, natural food markets, and holistic practitioners that they don't want to offer free copies of New Spirit Journal to their clients because people might get the "wrong idea." I am not sure what that means.

Others have quit offering the newspaper to their clients because their "Christian" customers complained. Instead of inviting them to bring their own publications in and offering their customers a variety of reading material, the owners decide not to offend the "Christians." They don't seem to mind offending those of us who are open spiritually and see all paths leading to the same place ultimately.

Ah, yes, those pesky Christians! It is sad that some of the more outspoken people of this faith get most of the attention and most of the press. Yes, I have some friends who are Christian and attend mainstream churches. Yet, they still have open minds and hearts. They realize that Jesus never started such a closed-minded and unloving religion as the one some people belong to and hang his name on.

    I like to say it is good that Jesus rose from his tomb because if he hadn't he would be turning over in his grave when seeing what people do in his name.

Let's network!

Of interest to me when I returned full-time to the world of metaphysical spirituality is how fractured the community had become. There wasn't a shared sense of mission that had existed in 1996. Again, this is probably due to the mainstreaming of many of the concepts and practices. However, I saw a need for more networking.

From my viewpoint, people needed to get together more and feel a sense of community and bonding. I had heard about some holistic chambers of commerce being started in other parts of the country and decided to start one in Seattle. Along with a few other people, we set up a non-profit, invited people to join, and started having meetings.

People loved the concept and we began to set up committees so we could start being active as an organization. After about a year, however, things stalled. We couldn't find enough people who were interested in doing the volunteer work necessary to build and grow such an organization. Many people wanted the benefits of such an organization but didn't feel they had the time to support it by volunteering. And the income wasn't enough to pay someone to be the director.

Eventually, I resigned, thinking that maybe if I pulled my energy out someone else would step up. Although the board of directors did their best, the volunteers didn't materialize and the organization was put on inactive status.

Around that time, we started a less formal lunch group called Good

Company. We met once a month, enjoyed lunch together, and networked. This continues to this day and there are now several groups in different areas. None of them are large which is actually good because it allows people to get to know one another. Many good referrals and assistance has come of these lunches. And, best of all, we have a good time!

I am a big believer in networking. In fact, that is really what New Spirit Journal is all about. It provides a place for people to connect through the written word – and spoken through our online audio interviews – and get to know one another. There are professional organizations, meet-up groups, and other such networking groups. This is one of the best ways I know to connect with other like-minded people. There's no reason to be a lone wolf anymore.

Voy a España.

One morning in 2007, two years after we started publishing New Spirit Journal, my telephone rang at 7:30 in the morning. Usually I wouldn't answer at that hour. My intuition said I should pick up the phone. So, I did.

A man introduced himself and asked if I spoke Spanish. I said I spoke a little but not enough to carry on a conversation with him on the phone. He said he would try to speak English and he did pretty good.

He said his name was José Luis and he reminded me that he was the man who had been publishing my writing in Spain since 1994. He and I had been students of the home-study course – Builders of Adytum, which teaches tarot, Kabalah, and other spiritual sciences (www.bota.org) – at the same time but had not met. A mutual acquaintance had made José aware of my first newspaper.

He had asked if he could reprint some of my articles from The New Times and I gave permission. He had been publishing my articles ever since.

José operates a spiritual school in Barcelona, Spain, and publishes a magazine and books. I hadn't thought about this for quite awhile but remembered when he reminded me. He said he was putting on a conference about the Kabbalah and wanted me to be a speaker. He said he would pay my expenses and a speaker's fee.

My first inclination was to say "No." Who was this man, really, and why would I want to go to Spain. My mother had always wanted to go to Spain but I had never even thought of going there. Something told me not to say no and to keep talking to José.

I told him I wasn't qualified to speak on the Kabbalah and he said that was fine. I could speak on anything I had written about, that his students loved my writing and as long as I spoke on those subjects, it would be fine.

I said I didn't speak Spanish well enough to give talks and he said

My wonderful publisher in Barcelona, José Luis, smiles as people in the audience request more women speakers in the future.

they would have an interpreter for me. I hesitated. He said he would send me an email with a link to their website and then I could decide. I agreed. It wouldn't do any harm to check this out further.

Within a few days, his email arrived with a link to his site. I was able to see photos from a similar event he had done the year before as well as information about the event coming up in a few months.

I looked over the offer he made and everything said I should accept and I did. It was a risk, of course. I didn't feel this was a scam, but what if the talks I gave weren't what José wanted? I was going to be the only woman speaker in an esteemed group of male professors and rabbis. What if my material didn't stack up to theirs?

What if I wasn't able to give good presentations with an interpreter. What if I didn't like Barcelona or the people didn't like me?

I overcame all my own objections, agreed to go, took Rhonda with me, and went.

What an experience it was! From the second I arrived until the moment I left, amazing things happened. José Luis and his students treated

My initial concerns about speaking at the Kabbalah Conference in Barcelona quickly dissipated as soon as I was giving my first talk with support from my translator Alex. The audience spoke Spanish, French, Portuguese, Italian, and English.

me like a queen, my presentations went beautifully, my interpreter and I clicked and worked together like we had one mind, and I love Barcelona. It is my new second home.

Over the next few years, José Luis published two of my books in Spanish and I returned twice to give weekend workshops to delightful students I still communicate with in various ways.

・・・・・

Rest Stop

Many times people have asked me how I made this happen and I always tell them I didn't make it happen. I live my life in a certain way and, as you have already read, this is only one of the fabulous things that have happened. Let me share some of what I did that influenced the outcome. Perhaps there will be something here to apply to your life.

1. I was willing to share my writing for many years without asking for compensation and this allowed the universe to return the bounty to me.

2. I followed my intuition and picked up the phone at an unusual hour when I really didn't feel like talking to anyone. I was available.

3. Even though the man on the phone spoke only a little English and I spoke only a little Spanish, I again followed my intuition and didn't hang up.

4. I was willing to step out into the unknown with no guarantee of how things would go. I was willing to risk being uncomfortable and maybe even greatly embarrassed if my talks didn't go well. I was able to let go of the undermining thoughts that I wouldn't be able to give as good a presentation as the other speakers.

5. At the time of the phone call, I had been doing a lot of releasing of unconscious emotions and blockages. I believe this had a lot to do with José even thinking of contacting me. After all, he had known of me for years and this was his second conference, not his first. Why did he call me this time and not the prior year?

6. I trusted the process. Every step of the way, from the first phone call to getting on the stage to speak in Barcelona, involved trusting. I was totally out of my element and was even speaking to an audience who, by-and-large, didn't speak English.

7. I have learned to be grateful for everything in my life, even the things I don't necessarily like. Sometimes our good is disguised as a challenge. If we are not grateful for the challenge and push it away from us, we could be rejecting something very special.

As Helen Keller said, "Life is either a daring adventure, or nothing at all." We can play it safe and live as we always have or we can be willing to step out, trust ourselves and life's processes, and see what sort of fabulous things are in store for us.

Sure, sometimes we might face some uncomfortable results, but my experience has been that, more often than not, when we say "Yes, and thank you!" to life we open the door to a grand adventure.

Try opening the door to a greater life by saying "Yes, and thank you" to life a little more often. The worst that can happen is you will have a great story to share with the rest of us.

My brother dies.

At the same time we were planning for my move from the senior center to working at New Spirit Journal full-time, my brother Lou was dying and because he did not have a partner or other family member to help, it fell to me.

Lou died alone. I think he wanted it that way. For a few years before he died, my brother had become an angry man. We were really close during childhood and for many years as adults. From the time we were children, we used to love to laugh together, to play jokes on one another.

Once we were both walking the metaphysical path, we were able to share many ideas and dreams with one another. He was two years older than I and studied metaphysical spirituality before I did. He even got to see Ram Dass speak in the early days of his career. Lou loved Sufism, the mystical branch of Islam, and spent time with a Sufi group in his younger days.

But then he became angry. He was angry about everything. Politics. Religion. His own life.

My brother loved music and was a musician. He played the piano, organ, and harpsichord. Sometimes he was paid for being a musician, such as when he was the church organist for various Protestant churches. But mostly, he had to make his living doing things he didn't like to do.

He plucked and cleaned chickens on a production line for awhile; a gruesome task I know went against every fiber of his being. He worked as a store clerk in music stores. He learned how to do commercial embroidery and was good at it. Lots of times he was without work and my mom would help him out financially. He worked at a school helping disabled kids. His final job was working in an adult family home helping disabled adults.

Lou was not happy, even though he loved the various people he worked with. He always felt he should be composing and playing his music, but could never figure out how to make it work for him. He literally died with his music in him.

Frequently, he would quote from the Bible: "Look at the lilies of the field. They neither toil nor spin and your father takes care of them." He would always add, "But they don't have to work as daisies in the meantime." Lou was mad at God and blamed God for his lack of ability to work in music full-time and support himself.

I tried to help him, especially once I became involved in metaphysics. I tried to steer him to teachings that could help him. He would try something awhile and then give up before it had a chance to work. Frequently, he walked around with a dark cloud hanging over him.

I'll never forget the time he came to visit me when I lived in Vancouver, Canada. We were walking around Granville Island and had sat down outside to enjoy an ice cream cone. He was telling me how horrible his life was. He didn't know where his rent would come from, he didn't have a job, and he felt he would never be able to do what he wanted to do. He said, "How can it get any worse than this?"

Just then a seagull flew over us and made a deposit right on my brother's head. I will never forget the look of absolute disgust and self-loathing I saw on Lou's face. Although we both saw the humor of the bird pooping on his head right at that moment, we were also sad because it truly did externalize how he felt about himself and his life.

Lou could be one of the most loving, generous, people I knew. Yet he could be mean, had a bad temper, and even had a very vicious tongue. In the last few years of his life, before we knew he had cancer, I stopped spending much time with him and he seemed to like it this way. He was difficult to be with because almost everything that came out of his mouth was angry.

He was angry at the government. He was angry at God. He was even angry with me. I quit taking his phone calls at one point and would let voice mail pick up when he called. I didn't want to hear his angry outbursts that were being fueled by alcohol. He knew I was screening my calls and one time he left a particularly vicious message telling me what a terrible person

I was for not picking up the phone.

I spoke with him shortly after that and explained that I paid for my phone service and that I had a phone for my convenience, not his. It was up to me whether I wanted to talk on the phone or not.

My brother drank. A lot. He also smoked cigarettes. When I also drank and smoked, we would have some fun times together. I quit smoking and only drank socially at that time – now I don't drink at all – so eventually we were on different paths when it came to substance use and abuse.

One day my brother came to see me at work and said he had just come from the dentist. Our parents had not raised us to take care of ourselves properly, so neither one of us went to the dentist often. He went far less often than I did so his teeth were in terrible condition. The dentist said his mouth was in bad shape and he wanted my brother to go to a specialist for a biopsy. Lou said the dentist wasn't sure but it could be cancer.

We were both stunned and, to be honest, I let myself go into denial about it. I figured I would wait and see what the doctor said before entertaining the worst. Deep inside, though, I knew I wouldn't be surprised to learn it was cancer.

That is exactly what it was: mouth cancer. It was already a stage four which is very advanced. The next few months, Lou had numerous doctor appointments and they decided to do major surgery. They would remove the cancerous tissue and bone from his mouth and replace it with bone and tissue they removed from his back. It was a horrible surgery to go through but they hoped it would result in removing all of the cancer.

He was sad and scared and angry about what was happening. It was difficult to talk to him because he became withdrawn. There were a few occasions when we were able to have some heart-to-heart discussions and he said that if he survived this he was going to get busy and make music his life. He said he thought he had gotten cancer because he was not living his life purpose.

At another time he said he might commit suicide rather than go through the pain of surgery. He told me if I was called and told he had driven his car off highway two going over Steven's Pass in Washington State, that he wanted me to know it was not an accident.

Instead, he did go through with the surgery and I helped him as much as I could, taking him to appointments and trying to help him when he came home. There were times, though, when it was very difficult to be with him or to help him because he pushed me away. It felt like he wanted me there when he needed help and otherwise he would prefer I not be around.

Believe it or not, once the surgery was over he started smoking and drinking again. I asked him about it and told him I couldn't believe he would do that after what he had been through. He shrugged his shoulders at me.

After awhile, it looked like the cancer was gone. Lou's face healed and he was able to eat mostly normally. He got back his sense of humor and said he felt like he was being given a second chance to live his life's purpose. He said he had decided to find a way to work with his music full-time even though he didn't know how. I supported him in this and said I was sure if he did that he would be a lot happier.

Within a few months, though, he started having difficulties with his mouth again. The cancer was back with a vengeance. Before very long, the doctor said that it was time for Lou to go on hospice, that he had only about five months to live.

When we received this news, we were in his doctor's office. Lou was standing beside me. He put his arm around me, leaned down and whispered in my ear: "I will be your angel once I am on the other side."

This was one of the nicest and sweetest things he had ever said to me. I gave him a squeeze in return. I realized he was ready to go. My part was to help him as best I could and to make his final months and days as easy and pain-free as possible.

And I did. He was not the easiest person to help. He had quit driving because he was taking all sorts of drugs and he didn't have anywhere to go that I couldn't help him. I stopped by his apartment every morning and evening on my way to work at the senior center and back home. Usually he was just sitting in a chair. I had given him some healing music to listen to, but usually he was just sitting in silence, dozing off.

One time he said he didn't understand why I stopped by twice a day. I explained it was because I wanted to be sure he was okay. What if he fell and was lying on the floor and couldn't get up?

I began to look into some sort of assisted living for him because it was becoming clear Lou needed more help than I could give him since we lived over 30 minutes away from one another. Moving in with him or him moving in with me were not options. I had a meeting with a social worker and she felt pretty sure there was a place in an adult family home where he could be moved. She said she would get back with me and let me know for sure in a day or so.

A few mornings later, I got a phone call from the local hospital. It was 7 a.m. in the morning. They said my brother had been in an accident and I needed to come to the hospital right away. I asked if they had the right person, that my brother was very sick and not driving. The nurse said, "Oh, he's your brother all right. He has cancer of the mouth, right?"

"Yes, I said," stunned. "What happened?"

"He was in a car accident on highway 203 heading towards Duvall. He isn't hurt badly but will need a ride home."

"I'll be there as soon as I can," I said.

My mind was racing while I got ready and drove to the hospital. I was shown which room he was in. When I walked in, Lou looked at me like a scared, disobedient little boy.

"Were you really driving your car?" I asked. He nodded affirmatively.

"What were you thinking?" I asked.

Because of the cancer in his mouth, he had difficulty speaking but he managed to tell me that he was hearing voices in his mind and they told him to drive to his place of employment.

Not knowing what to say, I just shook my head and helped him get ready so I could take him home. After having gotten him safely settled in, I went to get his car out of impound. It had been totaled and when I went to get it I learned it would cost $300 to get it and then I would have to have it towed somewhere else. I decided to let them keep the car. This would keep Lou from driving it again and the only fee would be the towing charge from the accident.

I drove back to Lou's apartment and told him what I thought we should do. He began to argue with me, saying he wanted his car back. When I started to explain that it was totaled and it would cost $300 to get it back plus a towing fee, he continued to argue with me.

The stress of everything finally caught up with me. I looked him in the eye, started crying and said, "I am trying to help you. There is no

Lou J. Gibson

one else who will do the things I am doing for you. For once, would you please just cooperate, sign over the title to your car and let me finish handling this? Quit making this so difficult."

He understood, signed the papers, and I left telling him I would be back the next morning to check on him. Everything was fine the next morning so I went in to work. That day I received a call from the social worker saying Lou could move into the adult family home that afternoon. I was relieved because it did not feel safe for him to live alone.

While in the midst of a meeting at the senior center, the receptionist came to me and said there was an emergency phone call. The local EMTs from the fire department were on the line telling me I had to come to my brother's apartment right away. They said he had been found wandering around in the middle of a busy street. He had to be quite a sight since his head was in white bandages.

Fortunately, I knew the medics involved due to my work with seniors. On numerous occasions at the assisted living facility, I had to call them to come and assist when someone had fallen or had some sort of physical problem. I said I had no idea what he was doing in the middle of the road, that he had been fine when I checked on him a few hours earlier, and that I had just received word I could move him to the adult family home that afternoon.

I promised I would stay with him and not leave him alone again. Had I not been able to do that they would have had to take him to the hospital. My brother could no longer be trusted to be alone.

He lived another two weeks. I saw him daily and some of his friends from work went to see him. Mostly, though, he slept. I took care of finding his cat a good home and emptied and cleaned his apartment for him.

A few days before he died, I was able to talk to him and told him how wonderful it would be for him to see our parents, other relatives, and friends of his who had passed over. He didn't open his eyes, but he was able to squeeze my hand.

The sorrow I felt about my brother's passing had more to do with feeling he had not accomplished his life's work here. I felt he was keenly aware of this and had decided to step out, spend some time in the spirit world, and perhaps return to try again at some point.

Rest Stop

One of the biggest lessons anyone can take from Lou's life is this. Whatever you feel is your life's talent, life's work, or life's calling, don't allow anything or anyone keep you from following it. Usually, the person who keeps us from this is ourselves. It is our own lack of self-worth, our own doubts, our own inability to accept our gifts and be willing to share them with others.

Are you doing what you feel called to do with your life? If not, why not? Who or what are you allowing to stand in your way? Whatever it is, now is the time to do whatever you need to do in order to get busy and follow your dreams.

We need you to do this. You have a part to play in this Earth-drama. Without you playing your part, the drama is incomplete. You are actually being selfish by not sharing your talents and gifts with the rest of us.

Sure, it can be difficult to follow your dreams. Look at some of what I went through in following my dream of publishing a spiritual newspaper. It was hard. There was not a lot of glory to what I did, nor to what I do today. Newspaper publishing is not a business with great financial rewards, especially these days when many publications are closing their doors due to lack of revenue. Most publishers are continually reinventing themselves to stay alive.

Why do we do it? Because it is our life's calling. Because we are providing a service in which we believe. You can do whatever it is you feel called to do. Accept your life calling. Decide to do it no matter what. Make a plan. Follow through even when the going gets tough. Ask for help. You will never be happy until you are on your life path so why not start today. Even if the first step is a simple one, why not do it now? You don't know what the future holds. You only have today. Make it one that will satisfy you at the soul level.

It's been nine years since my brother made his transition and we have kept in touch. Before he left we agreed that every time I see a rainbow I will know he is making contact with me, sending love and support. I see rainbows at some very odd times and always thank him for making contact with me.

Our loved ones who pass to other dimensions are closer to us than many people recognize or accept. They still care about us just as we do them. Some of them do pass along to a dimension where they attend schools of some type and maybe aren't always able to make contact with us. But as a general rule, it has been my experience that those we are closest to here on earth remain accessible if we reach out to them.

There's nothing to fear in doing this and a lot of possible great results, so reach out and see what happens.

Here's something I have shared with people that seems to be helpful. It's all about how to sabotage your own success. It is written with a bit of humor but everything is absolutely true. Do these ten things if you want to sabotage your own success!

Krysta's Top Ten Ways to Sabotage Your Success

10. Do not change any of your habits. Are your habits helping you or hurting you? In order to make the changes you say you want in your life, it might be necessary to make adjustments to your habitual way of doing things. If you really want to sabotage your success, stay attached to the way you do things now and refuse to change any of your habits.

9. Live in the past or the future; never the present. As long as you continue to rehash the past, you will remain stuck. And as long as you think your good is only in the future, you won't be able to be in the present where all good things happen. Do not live in the present and you can be sure you will not reach your goals.

8. Focus only on the outer rewards. You will never be satisfied if you keep your eyes only on the outer world, things like the new car, better job, or relationship. Don't pay any attention to your inner world, your soul quest, or inner visions and you will be sure to be unhappy.

7. Feel guilty as much as possible. You have probably done a lot of really wrong things so be sure to focus on them as much as you can. And when other people in your life try to make you feel guilty because you're not doing what they want you to do, be sure to give in to them and roll around in the guilt. This is a great way to

stay put in your life.

6. Be impatient. Try to always be in a hurry and push yourself to complete every project as quickly as you can. There's never enough time anyway, so just rush through life without giving yourself time to think or to be. The extra stress that impatience causes is sure to add to your defeat.

5. Fear change. Change is hard so do your best to fear it and avoid it at all costs. Fear is one of those emotions you can't get enough of so be afraid as much as you can and do not develop any sense of courage. Staying stuck in fear is a sure way to avoid reaching your goals and dreams.

4. Worry about what other people think of you. After all, it would be a shame if you were to be your own person, make your own decisions, and live your own life. Be sure to let other people's opinions, especially those closest to you, determine how you live your life.

3. Don't plan how to do whatever it is you say you want to do. Just figure things out as you go along. Don't sit down and decide how you will go about reaching your goals and don't reach out to anyone else for help in making your plans. Just flying by the seat of your pants is a certain way to stay right where you are.

2. Make excuses for why you can't succeed. As much as possible think of the ways it is not possible for you to succeed and then state them loudly and clearly as often as possible to as many people as will listen to you. People who fail are usually really committed to this.

1. Do nothing. Whine about how bad things are and continue to sit on the sidelines being jealous of the other people who are making efforts and changes in their lives. This is the single best way to sabotage any ideas you might have about improving your life.

Gurus.

In one of the articles I wrote during The New Times's days, I wrote that we don't need gurus because daily life is our guru. Since then I have changed that to say "daily life is our teacher." There is a big difference between a spiritual teacher and a guru.

Because of my work in the spiritual community, I have met many people who follow a particular teacher or organization. And I have met many who have a guru. I have interviewed people such as Ram Dass who openly follow their guru and share the teachings with others. I have always honored the guru-disciple relationship but didn't feel drawn to follow that path.

I suspect the reason is because of my experience in the convent. Jesus was our guru and is the guru of most Christians. We didn't use that word but the relationship is the same. For me, I had made a promise that I would never let myself be duped by a religious organization again.

It took me a long time to understand what a guru is – and isn't – and to finally accept having one in my life. Let me tell you how it happened for me.

For well over 20 years, the Ananda Church of Self-Realization and their businesses, the East West Bookshop and the Living Wisdom School, were a part of my work. They began advertising in The New Times and writing articles from time to time in the mid-1980s. I enjoyed knowing them and always felt a kinship with them. But I didn't pursue anything deeper than our working relationship.

I didn't pursue personal relationships with people from any organization after being criticized in the early days of The New Times. People seemed to feel I should not be involved with any organization so I could represent everyone equally. I agreed with that position and kept that policy when I started my first newspaper.

However, a few years ago several things happened to change this for me. First, I began to feel I would like to be involved with one spiritual group again. My work has enabled me to read about and study many different groups and spiritual ideas but, with the exception of the years I spent studying the Builders of the Adytum material, I never allowed myself to get involved with any one group or organization. I began to realize I missed going deeper into one particular practice or system and I missed having a deeper spiritual community.

My work with New Spirit Journal is about community, but this community is so diverse and so spread-out that it is difficult to be involved in any particularly deep way. I began to mentally cast around to see if I was drawn to any particular group or teachings.

Every year Ananda sends out Christmas cards and I was on their list and every year I received one. Several years ago, the card had an enclosed photograph of Paramhansa Yogananda. I took the photo and put it on a book shelf in the room where I meditate every day.

It sat there for a few years. One day as I walked past this photo, it fell to the floor in front of me. I put it back on the shelf. A few days later, it fell again. I put it back and was intrigued. Could this be a sign? When it fell a third time, I knew it was no accident.

I am not a person who has experiences of books falling onto her head in bookstores, so this photo falling right in front of me got my attention.

Not long after this, I saw that the Living Wisdom School was having an opening of their new thrift shop and went to the dedication ceremony. The spiritual directors of the local Ananda Church, Padma and Hriman McGilloway, were there. We visited a bit and I felt something different, but wasn't sure what was happening for me.

During this time I started writing a series of articles for New Spirit Journal. The articles were interviews with local church groups in which they could explain their beliefs and practices. I did this because I figured if I was looking for a spiritual community or home, probably others were as well.

When it came time to interview the Ananda organization, I was given the privilege of interviewing the founder, Swami Kriyananda. It was a telephone interview. We didn't meet face-to-face, but his delightful energy came through the phone line loud and clear. (You can hear this interview in the audio section of www.newspiritjournal.com.)

Next, I decided to go to Sunday services at Ananda. I had attended services at some of the other churches I interviewed, but had not attended one there.

I knew some of the people who were there that first Sunday I went and felt quite at home. The service was very devotional with chanting and spiritual readings, time for meditation, and, of course, a talk. I particularly enjoyed the various times the entire congregation would chant "aum" together. It was very powerful and filled with high energy.

The Ananda churches have a series of pictures hanging on the wall at the head of the church over the altar. The pictures are of Jesus, Lahiri Mahasaya, Babaji, Sri Yukteswar, and Yogananda. All men. What's up with that, I thought to myself?

Where are the women saints, the women gurus? Oh, no, have I fallen

"Who are these men who grace the front of the Ananda Temple," I wondered. "Don't tell me this is another spiritual organization that puts men first while the women cook and clean!" Over time, these fears were put to rest for me.

back into the dark ages where the leaders are all male and the women only serve in the capacity of helpmates? That would certainly not be for me. I had enough of that with the Catholic church, thank you very much.

Still, I felt drawn to the teachings of Yogananda and very drawn to the people I was meeting and to the energy of the church. I got a new copy of *Autobiography of a Yogi*, Yogananda's signature writing which has been read by millions of people. The edition I got was published by Crystal Clarity, the publishing arm of Ananda, and it is an unedited version of the original which was published in 1946.

I started reading more of Swami Kriyananda's books and listening to his recorded talks and I went to Sunday services when I could. I live over an hour from the closest Ananda center so I wasn't able to go as often as I would have liked.

Although I had meditated for over 30 years – and longer, if you count the five convent years – I was ready to study one particular method and see where it took me. I took the Ananda meditation course and began using it daily.

Not long after that, I took Raja yoga which is a three-month course that covers everything from meditation to chakras, breathing, Hatha yoga, and more. It was as if I was studying an intense course that included everything I had studied during the prior 30 years. I loved it.

The decision came whether or not to learn what is called Kriya yoga. Yogananda devotes an entire chapter to this meditative practice in his autobiography and he calls it "the airplane route to God." That sounded good to me! Part of the path to being taught this technique is becoming a disciple of Yogananda. Uh-oh.

Could I do this? Could I limit myself in this way? Was this a trick on the part of Ananda to tie me down to their one way of thinking, doing, and praying? And what the heck did I need a guru for? I seemed to be doing very well on my own.

One of the things I like about myself is that I am very open-minded and I am willing to change. In fact, not long ago my spouse commented on how I used to not like historical novels or movies. Now I enjoy them.

And I told her, "Yes, that's one thing I like about myself. I am willing to change!"

I turned to my heart and asked if this was the path for me and I got a resounding "Yes." By this time I had been studying enough to know who the five men on the altar were and why there weren't women there. I also saw how women play as important a role at Ananda as the men do.

The five men on the altar are the line of gurus followed by Ananda. The reason they are men is because at the time each of them was alive and teaching they couldn't have done what they did if they had incarnated as women.

Yogananda left India in the 1920s and traveled all over the United States teaching and building his organization. This could not have been done by a woman at that time. That work required a soul who was in a male body. It was a yang sort of job. The same is true of each of the others. This is the line of gurus Ananda follows. They were in male bodies but the teachings apply to everyone.

There is an interview about this that I did with Padma McGilloway at www.newspiritjournal.com in the audio section. She talks about this from her point of view. She has been with the Ananda Church for over 40 years and I hold her in high regard. And I have seen for myself that woman are treated equally. This has become a non-issue for me.

But a guru? Could I do this? Yes. And here is how my understanding has changed.

Imagine you want to climb Mount Everest. Would you go to the mountain climbing supply store, buy some gear and a few books, and then take off and try climbing the mountain on your own? I doubt it.

If you were going to become a surgeon, would you grab a few books about how to perform heart surgery and then hang out your shingle? Nope.

In both cases, not only would you need some very specialized training and studying, you would also want and need someone who had done it before and who was willing to be your teacher or guru. Wouldn't you feel honored if your teacher was a world-renowned mountain climber or heart specialist who was willing to share their expertise with you?

And what if they were willing to actually walk beside you up that mountain or stand with you the first time you cut someone open? Wouldn't that be grand?

This is what the guru does. In this case, the goal is finding God, realizing our oneness with God. The guru has been there, is there, and is willing to share not only the how and the why but is willing to lend you his or her energy to help you.

This isn't a case of someone telling you what to do, lording it over you, or restricting you. It's someone being willing to share what works with you and save you a lot of stumbling around on your own. It's deeper than this, but this gives you the gist of what I'm talking about.

I took discipleship and I studied Kriya yoga, which I have now been doing for several years. There are various kinds of Kriya yoga. They are not all the same. If you decide to pursue this as a spiritual practice, be sure to investigate throughly before choosing which path to walk down.

Some people teach this technique over a weekend and others, such as Ananda, require about a year's preparation. Good things take time. Kriya yoga is a very powerful technique. Personally, I would want to be sure my mind, body, and spirit were properly prepared for the amount of energy being moved through me.

For the record, I am not the world's best disciple. I do my best to study and to learn and to practice what I am taught. I meditate daily and have done so since that first visit to the meditation doctor in 1983. But I don't do everything perfectly and I know this is okay. Sure, sometimes my good Catholic girl raises her hand and wants me to feel guilty about something. Usually, I can get her to put her hand down and relax.

At Ananda one of the words used is "directional." We might not do things perfectly. We might have our slip-ups. What counts is our sincerity and efforts in the right direction; thus, it is a directional path. It is a process.

Like life itself, spirituality is a process, not an end game, at least not in this world it isn't! It is important to have a path to follow and to do our best to be committed to it for the long haul. There are many enlightened spiritual groups and churches to choose from today. No one has to be alone on the path. Be open to finding a spiritual home and family. Many wonders await you there.

Afterword
or What a journey we've been on.

This has been quite a journey, hasn't it? And like your life journey, mine is continuing as well. As I'm writing this, we've made the decision to stop printing New Spirit Journal and go green by having an online journal instead.

This was quite a decision and has once again propelled me along an expanded path with new learning and spiritual growth. It's sad because I have been involved in publishing print newspapers for 30-plus years. However, it is exciting because this means we're part of the digital age, helping the planet by having a more neutral carbon footprint.

If there is anything I hope you can take away from my life stories, it is this:

You are here for a reason. I know sometimes you might doubt this and I know that sometimes you might feel you are facing insurmountable odds that are not in your favor. I know there are times you probably ask yourself what is the point of it all.

When this happens, I want you to sit down and take a good look at your life to-date. Maybe even write your life story. Look for the threads. Look for the clues. Look for the apparent coincidences. In those you will find the answer to why you're here. One of your biggest purposes is to be yourself, your true self, and to let your work in the world flow from this higher or superconscious self.

Once you've discovered your reason for being here, please make the commitment to live your purpose. Get the information or training you need. Gather up your courage. Deal with whatever issues are placed in your path.

Whatever sorts of challenges are given to you, embrace them and know they can take you to new levels of understanding if you allow this to happen. If your life purpose changes, be willing to travel in new directions. In today's world, it is not uncommon for people to express their life purpose in multiple ways.

We need you more than ever. Without you giving service by living your purpose, the planet will not be whole. Never for one instant doubt how important you are to the planet, the universe, and, yes, to God.

God created you for a reason, and now it is up to you to be the best you possible so that reason will be fulfilled. If you ever doubt this, if you ever doubt you can do what you came to do, look back at my life. Look at the improbable situations, people, and circumstances that were thrown in my way.

If I could summon the strength and courage to face what I faced – if others who have faced far more challenging situations than I have could do it – so can you!

I've designed a guidance deck that I think can help you along the way. I've based it on the various situations I've seen in my life and in the lives of my clients. Using the deck can help when you get stuck or need insights. It can give you focus and receive guidance when you need it. Find the Anything is Possible Guidance Deck at your local bookstore, or through my website www.krystagibson.com after autumn 2015.

I hope to meet you someday. Come to a book signing or one of my classes. Send me an email. Friend me on Facebook. In today's world, there is no reason for us not to connect. Let me know what you're doing and how you're living your life purpose! And if I can help you with a Wisdom Reading or a Mentoring session, I would be delighted.

More information about me, my services, and various products can be found at www.anoasisforyoursoul.com or www.krystagibson.com And be sure to visit www.newspiritjournal.com where many wonderful articles, audios, and videos are offered 24/7. Sign up for my email lists at both websites so you can receive my weekly inspirational emails and notifications of various events of interest.

Wishing you the best and seeing you surrounded by angels,
Krysta Gibson
June 2015

Acknowledgements

To all the teachers, guides, and helpers, seen and unseen, I've had over the years: thank you!

To the loyal readers of my publications, books, and articles who have given awesome feedback, encouragement, and, yes, criticism: thank you!

To everyone who has participated in my newspapers: advertisers, volunteers, columnists, distributors, printers, postal and UPS workers: thank you!

To my family and friends, your support has meant everything to me: thank you!

To Rhonda Dicksion, my spouse, friend, co-creator, and co-parent to our delightful canine children: thank you!

And, finally, to you, dear reader. I appreciate you more than you will ever know: thank you!

www.ingramcontent.com/pod-product-compliance
Lightning Source LLC
LaVergne TN
LVHW052100090426
835512LV00036B/2920